BR[] FREE

From Your

HAMSTER WHEEL

Your travel itinerary to
professional fulfilment

HULYA KURT

Cover image by: Noel Sellon, 99 Designs
Book design by: SWATT Books Ltd

Printed in the United Kingdom
First Printing, 2022

ISBN: 978-2-9701602-0-5 (Paperback)
ISBN: 978-2-9701602-1-2 (eBook)

Published by: Hulya Kurt
GENEVA, SWITZERLAND

www.innkick.com

TABLE OF CONTENTS

INTRODUCTION

Why did I decide to write a book about career progression? And specifically, about business professionals in the middle of their careers?

I have observed, during my professional life, that so many of my peers and colleagues feel stagnant after a while and have started to complain that no one sees them, their manager does not recognise their efforts, and that their job is getting boring.

I could see in all this a loss of motivation, a sapping of energy and the depressing feeling that this was how it is and will be and that one has just to live with it. In the meantime, these family responsibilities had increased. Maybe they have mortgages, children or need to take care of their elderly family members.

So, any changes that carry risk like, looking for a new job or becoming self employed or independent, all these no longer seem viable options.

To verify this assumption, I conducted some interviews, calling out for volunteers on LinkedIn, Facebook and Instagram.

You might wonder if I received some responses. Well, I did and guess what, from a diverse slate of people. Those responding came from different countries and continents – from Africa, Europe and the Middle

East. People with different backgrounds and different positions. Here is a selection of five of the interview results and outcomes.

The first one is from Salome, in Africa: 13 years in the same bank. Same grade as when I started, it is boring, like a robot. I want to quit, have applied for many internal jobs, shortlisted but never getting any of them. It is about who knows who – the hiring managers has always got preferred candidates. You need to create your network with the managers who go out and have a drink. It should be that automatically you will be moved from entry level to next after 3 years at least. You have all the capabilities and experience but still the internal application system does not allow you to move up. Applying for other jobs now.

Flora, in Switzerland: I have reached the top of the learning curve, it has become repetitive, and I am lacking visibility although I know I can do more. No one trusts you and managers give you tasks which are low profile. Contracts are short term.

- Low self-development: I have reached the limit of my learning curve for my role and my work has become repetitive
- Increased visibility: I want to demonstrate my other skills to team members, project managers and senior management, to see my potential and understand that I can do more...
- Need to feel valued and recognized
- Afraid of the unknown: I have found my balance in the current team and have my comfort zone. The team understands that I am reliable, professional and can deliver. Starting a new role in a new organization would require demonstrating my capacity again before gaining credibility.
- Work-life balance: finding a role that would balance family life with children and a husband; and the work requirements.
- Finding a focus of further development after completing my first Master's degree and working many years. For example, learning to teach French as a Foreign Language vs. MBA.
- Finding a niche after my MBA programme: it was not clear what industry to focus on with so many different skills
- Contract vulnerability
- Racial discrimination

To overcome these challenges, I have increased my skills by completing more project management certifications, volunteering for additional tasks at work, participating in a mentoring programme, exploring other job opportunities, proactively discussing my career progression with my direct supervisor, gaining the team trust by demonstrating my reliability and professionalism, and increasing communication with others to know more about my interests and profile.

Nihan, in Turkey: My advice is as follows. In the beginning, a personal strategy is missing, but you don't think about it. Then you see others doing better, and at first you think it is the company, the manager and not you. First you need to be aware that you are responsible for yourself and no one else. You need self-awareness, as how you can be happier at work, is important. What have you done and what makes you happy? Goal setting is important for yourself, otherwise you feel you are a machine and have no influence. Articulate your desires openly, get involved in being part of volunteer groups, in the company and outside; talk to people around you to create your own network.

Dorcie, in Africa: I was laid off as a teacher. After so long stagnating in the same position, nobody is willing to promote you, nobody sees you. And then, in your most productive years, you find you are overlooked. You ask for the resources to gain qualifications but get rejections. So, I've taken the decision to start an MBA in International Affairs. Suddenly, you don't have the pressure to perform for others, as you are doing it for yourself.

Aydan, in Switzerland: I knew I had transferable skills but I always stayed in the same job role, the first I chose, that of business development manager. I had a fear of not finding anything else, but then slid by accident into finance, into a job I do but don't like. I've never taken time for myself and have always thought that I need to work on anything I was offered. I lacked the confidence to believe what I was doing was ever good enough, not trusting in my own abilities and skills. Now in fact it is getting better, as I have found that networking is important.

From these conversations, and many others, it became apparent that there is a major problem out there. A problem that exists but no one dares talk about it. Not you nor those running the company.

Although the main responsibility lies with you to drive forward your career, we must also acknowledge that company culture is equally important. If you are in a toxic environment where employees get bullied, it is not safe to speak up, you might run the risk of being labelled as difficult or too demanding. Or where career progression is only happening to the best buddies of the manager or CEO, if there is a bias towards the same background, culture or ethnicity, then that becomes a real barrier for being able to progress in the company.

Conclusions

In such environments, the best option is to find a new company. Intimidating or bullying environments are just not sustainable in the long run. Neither for your health and nor for your mental state.

You will feel frustrated, your values violated, you will start hating your job and ultimately burnout might happen.

To change jobs is not easy but it is possible.

That's the reason I started to write this book. To show you the way to get off your hamster wheel.

If you do have a satisfied, empowering work environment, then it is easier to manoeuvre within your company to show yourself in the right light. However, even in a company with diverse culture and is fostering employees' engagement, some career progression aspects can be neglected or not have thought put into them.

This is where this book aims to help you – to craft, step-by-step, your own career the way you want it to be.

There is a lot of emphasis on "you want it to be" as there is no such thing as perfect. But you can get closer or even achieve your ultimate goals. It is all up to you, seeing things from your perspective.

We all have thoughts of making a change, but we push them away and try to convince ourselves that what we have now is enough. You have a monthly salary; you have a job at least – some people of course don't even have a job. You comfort yourself and so do your family and your friends. They might say:

"Hey, you work at a good company, you have the guarantee that your salary will be paid and if the job is not exactly what you would like to see after so many years, this is not a dramatic problem."

Yes, they are right as well, it is not dramatic, and it is not the end of the world, but it is something you can change.

However, it is you who needs to decide whether it is important enough to set about creating a change in your career.

A question for you:

On a scale from 1-10, 10 being the highest, how important to you is your day-to-day job?

If your answer is 7-10 then it is very important, to you and as such, it is important that you are happy in it, if not, you may well need to make a change.

The change you choose to make does not need to be huge. It can be arranging to take on additional responsibility, becoming the deputy, or taking on an interesting project to stimulate and remotivate you in your job.

You probably spend more time at work than at home and with your family. Either at home or physically at your workplace. Therefore, it is paramount that you are satisfied with it.

If you are unhappy or suffering in your current position or company and yet day-in, day-out you need to go to work, then you need to take a hard look at your situation. You are probably not performing well, your attitude will be negative all the time, you may not have a good relationship with your peers and managers. You may not even care anymore, for you it is now only important to show up. You may even seek every opportunity to be on sick leave.

This is not fair to you, your employer and your teammates. So, be honest with yourself and with others and take steps to get out and move on. To relieve yourself and others.

This book will explain and show techniques that you can apply immediately. It focuses on mindset and attitude. Mindset is the key to start making changes. And, whatever you read here is not going to help you if you don't take action immediately.

I recommend that after each chapter, you make some reflection notes. Think about what you can do immediately, before you move on to the next one. Or, if you want to read the whole book first, then make sure that you review the book from A-Z and create your action plan.

Your time is too precious to be spent on something that you will not implement afterwards.

I would like you to avoid doing this. It is like attending a workshop. You get inspired, you think yes, I am going to do this and that. However, after going back to your day-to-day work, you soon forget about it, as your brain is programmed to go back to your old habits.

For that not to happen you need to be conscious. Make a daily note, a place holder of 30 mins every day to say: reflect, take action. Or whatever is a good prompt for you to step back and think and write.

If, like me, you are in the middle of your career, and so busy all the time, this is likely to resonate with you. You need to make time to think!

Create your pledge to yourself... your own personal promise.

Make it a simple one, something easy that is not overwhelming.

And create affirmations for yourself.

An affirmation confirms the belief that you can be, do and have whatever you want in your life.

Some simple rules apply to affirmations:

Personal: Describe a specific quality that you want, for example, "I build rapport and empathy with everyone I meet".

Positive: State what it is you want, rather than what you don't want. "I want enough money" rather than "I want no debts".

Use the present tense: "I am a manager" rather than "I will be a manager"

Believe in yourself: If you don't do that then no one will. Neither your manager nor your friends, nor people that you would like to work with.

You have the required skills: You are worth it. And if you don't have the required skills, then you have the grit and power to learn new skills.

You can do anything you want.

CHAPTER 1

KICKSTART YOUR CAREER

You have just finished school or an internship, or maybe have completed a qualification or a certain institution. You have found a job, and that has been challenging enough in itself, and you are so happy. Yes, that is what we feel when we have found our first real job. Put aside part-time jobs to support you during studies or to pep up your pocket money. I mean the job you deem as your first real job.

You are introduced to your team; you start to learn. Everything is new. Do you remember those times? These were so exciting, right? Someone is teaching you what you need to do, and what you are responsible for. Larger companies provide formal induction or onboarding processes to give you information about the company, policies, departments and what your duties are. Or you might have been assigned some mandatory online training.

Meeting new people

They come into your world, and you start to create connections. Firstly, with your buddy and your peers. Not to forget your direct manager. You are taking part in team meetings and people have started to get to know you and vice versa. Assuming you are already within your career, you have done this face-to-face. Or if you are new in your career, all this might be initially online, where the human touch is getting a bit lost, so I hope you will have had the opportunity to visit the office and see your real teammates.

You go out for lunch, coffee, and start to hear the office gossip. This is how you learn the on-site, true dynamics of the organization. How do managers react, what do people say, who is always sick, comes late to work, and who is hanging out with whom? Basically, you test the waters and are all ears.

Once you have started to know more, you also contribute with your 5 cents to the conversations, and you start being invited out for outings, drinks and become an integral part of the team.

You have quickly identified who you like hanging out with, as in each company there are little friendship circles, formed by intuition and common interests. And you are now part of it all and feel happy. You feel accepted, part of the family.

Do you remember these good times? Look back at your timeline and your memories.

Becoming an expert

Here is a likely journey as you make progress in your job. After several months, you start to get to know all the processes, your clients, and you know exactly what you need to do. It becomes a comfortable daily habit to switch on the PC and start working through your emails and tasks. You participate in meetings, can contribute confidently and people have started to come to you for advice. This has become your company, your team, your area of expertise. Your manager might start to give you ad hoc projects. You perform, give your best and you receive your reward, in monetary form or with promotion to a higher position. You might now be a manager, have people reporting to you or be an expert, a specialist in your domain, where you are pulled into global projects and initiatives. It feels too good to be true. You enjoy it, although it is stressful from time to time. You work overtime, sometimes to accommodate different time zones but you feel OK doing that. Ultimately, you believe in your company.

You also travel a bit, and it is exciting to travel on the company's cost. I always enjoyed this in the beginning, as you meet different peers in different countries, you socialize even more as you don't have any on-site responsibilities. These trips might even feel like a short holiday, to be away from home.

You now advance a bit more in your career, vertically or horizontally. Your performance speaks for itself. You are giving presentations to senior stakeholders; you lead your team and walk the talk. You feel recognized and appreciated in the company.

You are invited for after-work or dinner events by your manager during visits from executive leaders. You create rapport and trusting relationships with your key stakeholders and senior management in the organization. How rewarding is all this? It's cool, and you start to think, "I am in the right place".

This is what I was thinking at those points in my career as well. I was proud of myself that I had proven that I could deliver, and I had gained credibility and visibility in the eyes of my management.

On the flipside, at this point you have needed to work even harder to meet your growing expectations and the expectation of your managers. But you did not feel overwhelmed, as you are doing everything with excitement, and you are now in the wonderful habit of delivering more and more. You don't even realize that you are doing this – it's all just in line with your increased expectations.

During year-end performance reviews, you score highly and above average, and you are appreciated by your peers and colleagues.

Your decision-time

Fast forward, years passed by and you have your routine, day-in day-out and then suddenly it dawns on you. You seem to have become invisible. You cannot remember the last time that you were promoted in any way, shape or form, and your manager no longer recognizes your work. No new projects, no salary increase. Average performance reviews. In the meantime, your manager might have changed, and you might not get along. It appears to be a constant battle. Slowly, you start to lose faith in your organization and its management. It's not as it was before. The fun has gone, you are not growing anymore, you are not learning anything and there are no opportunities. The values and mission of the company have changed over time. Each year there is a new slogan, and you can no longer identify with the company. You have difficulty in motivating yourself to wake up and go to work. Specifically, after weekends. Sunday evenings turn into a torture. Even the thought makes you tired and nervous, which has an impact on your relationships with family and friends. You can't enjoy the moment, as you are always thinking about the next day. In some scenarios, you even call in sick to gain some relief for one or two days. However, these temporarily measures are not sustainable.

In such times, breaking out of your habit feels scary. You don't take action, as you are afraid of the answers or consequences that you are going to give yourself.

You are like an ostrich, putting its head in the sand but its butt is out there to be bitten. You can't escape the truth. The truth, that you are not happy anymore – everything is frustrating, and processes and policies are now always getting in the way of your creativity or improvement ideas. No one listens to you. Your manager has a certain way of thinking that isn't aligned with you and is not willing to help you to understand or develop yourself. Your peers might be feeling OK, even fulfilled at work. But you are unique. You have your own experiences, knowledge, thoughts and ideas. You don't need to be feeling the same as everyone else.

All this is absolutely OK and there is no right or wrong. What we want to discover here is what you exactly want and need to meet your emotions and expectations and what will make you feel fulfilled.

My own experience? I have felt bored or frustrated from time-to-time as well. During my 32 years at the same corporation, this was expected and perfectly normal. Although I occupied many different roles and had some interesting projects and was actively part of initiatives such as the Diversity and Inclusion Global Steering Committee, facilitated career workshops for employees, and organized fun events such as summer parties and wine tasting, I felt blocked and that I was no longer aligned with the company.

How did I cope with this? For me, it was obvious that I would like to stay at this company. That was the first decision I made. So, I had to look at what else was happening in the company that I could be part of, that would give me the boost, energy and adrenalin that I needed to perform at my best and feel acknowledged. I was reading each week the newsletters and news about my company, I attended 'town hall meetings' where our senior managers were talking and giving us updates. Once I spotted an opportunity, something new which was coming up, I approached the respective manager directly to seek either for a face-to-face short conversation or I would send an email and even ask for a meeting over the phone or Zoom, to express my interest. I even pestered my direct manager to be part of a new initiative or project that was about to kick off. Sometimes this worked, sometimes it didn't. If it didn't work, I would be down for a short while but would then pump myself up again. It was me who needed to act and no one else. So, I continued with my regular job but had a helicopter view, had all my senses open to seize any opportunity to change. It was like being an eagle, flying over a big field and waiting for the right occasion to grab the right opportunity.

Determination is the key to success

Depending on decisions you take in such situations, and we will cover how to make that decision in the right way in the next chapters, you create your own reality. Believe in what you want to achieve.

"What the mind can conceive and believe, the mind can achieve." A nice quote from Napoleon Hill.

In the world of NLP, neuro linguistic programming, the brain's so-called 'Thinker' can be primed to believe in your success. You have the power of your brain, and you don't and should not accept the status quo. The situation that you are in now is not forever. Everything can change and you don't know what the next day will bring.

The first step is to acknowledge that you don't feel good at work and that you want to change.

Start your day with one of the affirmations we mentioned in the Introduction.

Create your own mantra. The more you repeat it, the more you will believe in it. You need to train your unconscious mind, as it lies as the foundation under your logical mind and it is your powerhouse. To fuel your powerhouse with the right ingredients it is essential to be mentally prepared. Believe in yourself and your skills. You have a unique value proposition. You just might not know it yet. But everyone has one. And we will be looking at this in more detail in the next chapters.

This is a process, as such, sometimes it will take longer, sometime shorter. It may be like a rollercoaster, with ups and downs and a river winding left and right. It might be dark like in a tunnel, and then you see a glimmer of light at the end of it, so you need to make a decision which way to go. Imagine you are on a train, and you have started your journey. But without a destination, where will the train be going? Will it derail? Certainly, it will if you are not sure about your goal. Once the goal is set, the path to get there can be paved. How? Step by step. It is important though to start not to stand still, as change can only come if you act. Remember, you and no one else is in the driver's seat of your professional life. That initiative for its future direction lies with you, not your manager or the organization.

It will not be an easy path and you will feel uncertain at times, fearing that you are taking incorrect decisions. Not only for yourself but also people around you. It is a big responsibility, but if the result of making a change will be that you will be fully aligned with your inner self and your work, this will have an enormous impact on your personal life, and everyone around you will benefit from you being happy.

When we embark on a plane, what do the security rules say? First, put an oxygen mask on yourself and then help others.

So, what are you waiting for? It is time to take care of yourself. If your body, mind and soul are in harmony, your life will be flowing.

CHAPTER 2

FEELING STUCK ON THE HAMSTER WHEEL

You have moved up to a certain level in your career and are happy with what you have achieved. However, you start to feel that something is missing but can't put your finger on what is wrong.

This is normal, as we all have our daily responsibilities that can take up our day. We know them inside out and it feels comfortable to be in this situation. You have your monthly salary, your boss is satisfied with your work, you have your peers/colleagues that you socialise with, do sports with, run, go out for lunch and for a drink.

Every moment, every second, every meeting is familiar and this feels OK. You get your monthly paycheck and have security.

As comfortable as this is, it is getting boring. There is no excitement anymore. You feel that you are missing the opportunities to grow, to learn, to strive for a challenge. Moreover, it seems that no one notices you anymore. You feel invisible, you feel you don't have an impact and make a difference. Whatever you repeatedly do does not give you satisfaction anymore.

You may even have a manager that you cannot get along with but bear the situation as you are afraid to get out of your comfort zone.

It might feel to you that your colleagues and people around you seemed friendlier, more supportive and caring everyone was more friendly, sharing and caring but now it feels that you are just a number and don't have any great value. It feels like it has become a toxic environment.

Your hamster wheel

How do you feel? Trapped? Stuck? Like on a hamster wheel, you run and run but you are not going anywhere in your professional life. No promotion, no development, no assignment to difference projects, no salary increase and just an average year-end performance review. Was that it, you ask yourself. What else can I do? At the same time, you are afraid to ask to get out of your bubble, as in it there is a risk. In the short term, it is OK not to take action. You might have family to look after. Children that need to be picked up from school, the cost of maintaining home and much more. But it gets more and more difficult for you to wake up in the morning and find the motivation within. You are only going through the motion to get paid. You have lost interest in your organization or profession. More than that, it is becoming a nightmare. You start to worry from as early as Sunday afternoon that you need to go to work. You are thinking already about the backlog, the meetings and the stress that this creates.

Sounds familiar?

What is your urge to change?

Yourself. You don't feel satisfied. It bothers you deep down inside. Your misalignment has an impact on your emotions and an impact on your friends, family and anyone around you. You may seem to be less tolerant, start to get angry easily and impatient at people. It is not your intention to do so, but as you are not in line with your values and your work, this is the outcome. Put simply, you are not happy, and this unhappiness is projected around you.

So, what should you do?

Although this is easier said than done, you need to get out of your box. How, is the question. How to create a way forward that fits with you as a unique person. You can change in small ways or undertake a larger change. In both scenarios, you need to make a decision. Let's explore the foundation of our existence.

What are your values?

When in doubt, get your values out.

We are growing, we are changing constantly as human beings, that's why our values and our priorities change as well. This is the normal evolution of human beings.

Before we delve into values, let's look into the definition of values:

Values are basic and fundamental beliefs that guide or motivate attitudes or actions. They help us to determine what is important to us. Values describe the personal qualities we choose to embody to guide our actions; the sort of person we want to be; the manner in which we treat ourselves and others, and our interaction with the world around us. They provide the general guidelines for conduct.

They are the core of your soul, your mind, your North Pole.

So, let's conduct a value elicitation exercise, starting by asking yourself, "What is important for you in life?" And continue asking this question repeatedly until you have a minimum of 6-7, and then up to 10 values listed. You can ask anyone else for help to answer this question, it needs to be someone who is neutral.

Some examples of values:

Respect – integrity – freedom – belonging – purpose – authenticity

Continue by checking if any of the values listed can be regrouped or consolidated into themes. Once you are happy with your listed values, start to ask yourself which of these values are more important than others, now prioritize them top-down to create a hierarchy of your most important values.

We, as coaches, quite often use the Wheel of Life. You can find many versions of this on the internet, to download and complete. Here is an example of what one might look like when completed, having given a score out of 10 to each of the eight areas of your life. Complete one now as a snapshot of where you are in your life and your career now. Then, complete another one at a point in the future which reflects when you believe you will have made some significant changes. This might be in six months' time or perhaps one year from now. Use it as a way to see the progress you have made in achieving greater balance in your life. A version is shown as Activity 4 in the appendices.

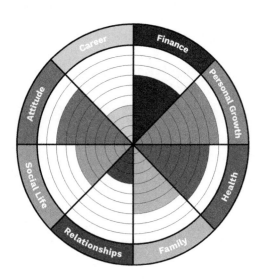

Why is this value exercise so important as a first step? Because if your work is not aligned with your values, you will feel frustrated all the time. Your work will be in conflict with your legacy, your GPS, your North Star.

Some people can live with some mismatches with their values and can find a way to compromise, that's also OK. It is your decision. You decide how to live. Don't forget, you create your own reality.

Now you have your top values listed. Examine them carefully, re-evaluate them if need be. To be sure about your values choice, sleep on it and review them next day. You can re-do this exercise as many times as you wish at any given time. And your values can change over time, as responsibilities change and we gain more experience. Life has an impact on us and our perspectives do change.

Now you have got your values, what's next?

What are your strengths?

I know, from coaching experience, that this exercise can feel time-consuming. However, taking time for yourself is precious and is so important. To take a step back, assess your inner self to help you to make good decisions.

What are your strengths? Do you know them? Have you ever listed them? Create a list of skills that you believe you possess.

We are focusing on your strong points rather than weaknesses, as these are the ones you can easily apply, and it is fun for you to use them. Once you are aware of your skills, think about how many of them you use in your day-to-day job. All of them, some of them or none?

If you are using none of your skills, it seems we have a challenge, as every day you will be feeling reluctant to go to work, as it has become torture for you. If you are using some of them, you are living with a compromise, and you may be happy to live with that. If you are using all your skills, you are extremely fortunate. However, this may mean that you are fulfilled and happy.

So, what should we do? Ask yourself the most difficult question: do you want to continue as is or are you now ready for a change to live a better life at work? Remember, we spend most of the time working, thus feeling happy at work is essential. There is no such thing as the perfect job. What does perfect mean anyway? Perfectionism does not exist as such, as there is always room for improvement or better ways of doing things.

Coming back to our initial question. Could you answer it? Yes, it is a hard question but worthwhile to consider. Do you need to change, because you are not using any of your strengths and none of your values are met? You are the only one who can answer that. It is normal that you don't want to change anything. Maybe it is not the right time, maybe it is not the right moment.

There is no one-size-fits-all and so, don't feel that there is anything wrong with you. However, remind yourself – do you want to really continue as is, even if this is impacting you in a negative way at work mentally and physically, and in your personal life as well? Is it affecting relationships with your family and friends and most importantly yourself?

"We want to change." Yes, but how? Let's crack on exploring the steps to take:

Creating a vision board

What is a vision board? It is a visual reflection of how you would like to live as your ideal future self. You can create your vision board by painting or drawing it yourself, finding images online that represent your ideal job or environment, or you can cut out pictures from magazines and paste them onto a large sheet of paper.

It is up to you what method and type fits you. Why is this so important? Because it is a poster that you will place in front of you. "You get what you expect" and this is how you can manifest your future with your vision board. This is a powerful way of putting your goals into action. You know 'goal setting'? Of course you do. You have team goals, company goals and your employee goals. However, we never think about our own personal goals in the context of writing them down or visualizing them. Whatever gets written, gets done. With that in mind, your vision board is the projection of your future state. You can create separate vision boards – one for your work and career, and one for your leisure, personal life, or you can combine all this into one. For the sake of this exercise, let's focus just on your professional life. You can create a vision of your profession, your job title and your office. It might be that you want to be an entrepreneur. Why limit yourself in the corporate world?

Other questions to ask yourself: What would I do as work if there were no constraints such as money or responsibilities? What would be my ideal profession? And what would I not like to regret, when I sit on a bench at age 80? Life is too short to miss out on opportunities or tries. What could be the worst consequence if I don't try? What will I gain if all goes well?

Plenty of vision board examples can be found on the Internet. As part of the appendices, I have attached mine, see Activity 5.

Now you have created your vision board and you know where you want to get to. Still the question remains on how to get there.

My career in brief

To help to illustrate some of the dilemmas and decision-making points you may come across, I would like to tell you a bit about my career story.

I don't have any MBA, PhD or even a university degree. I started with the multinational company Reuters in 1989, back when there were no PCs and no Internet or mobile. This already feels unbelievable, right?

I started as a sales secretary, typing away on a typewriter. After a while, familiar with the job, I started looking to see how I could help and so put my nose into customer administration, as they needed help. The business was booming – Reuters was the one and only financial and news information provider back then. No competition, can you imagine? So, I got the offer to move to customer administration as their assistant. From then onwards, I raised my hand to anything new which was coming along and was soon regarded as an expert with a wide range of skills. I started to travel for business and training, and I enjoyed every bit of it. Slowly but surely, I moved up the ladder, from team manager, to business admin manager and got the offer to move to Geneva in 2005 with my family, to lead the Customer Order Management team for a huge region of 80 countries. In the meantime, I did my PMP (Project Management Certification) and Management ILM (Institute of Leadership and Management) certifications. I moved on either horizontally or vertically. Did I get what I wanted all the time? Not at all. I applied for some positions where I was not taken on, and I got frustrated and angry... and lost my motivation. I carried on working but at times only contributed the bare minimum. And then I picked myself up to carry on and find other ways of getting myself energized. Some new projects were assigned to me that I could lead, and that kept me going.

To conclude, after 32 years, I was made redundant. Another milestone, another decision to take.

And I decided not to stay in corporate life anymore but now here was the opportunity to follow my passion. Helping people to find their way in this business jungle. Coaching. My redundancy occurred just before the pandemic, so this was a great time to start studying. I was able to gain my coaching diploma and accreditation, and I worked on developing my network in the coaching world.

So, what are the key takeaways from the whole story?

I learned a great deal from these experiences. One essential learning is, never give up. Make your decision. Be curious and courageous. Do remember that sometimes you need allow time for yourself, your manager, your leader.

However, if things carry on to the point that you can't take it anymore, it is time for concrete action.

Whatever your decision might be, now it's time to make it – staying in the same organization, moving to a new industry, moving to be self-employed or maybe even taking a break for a while.

Let's recap

You have your values.

You have your strengths.

You have your vision board.

How do you combine all the above into an action plan?

And, most importantly, have you reached your decision already? What do you want to do?

- Stay in the same organization and find ways to move on, either horizontally or vertically?
- Stay in the same organization, don't do anything and continue as is?
- Change company but stay in the same industry?
- Change company AND industry?
- Become independent and self-employed?

Check which one of these resonates with you the most. Are you now in a position to make up your mind?

Whatever the result and decision, now it's time to act. Believe in yourself – you're not the first one to make such a change and you won't be the last either. You might have been jealous of those friends who have taken such a leap of faith. Now it's you who will be doing it.

At this point, positive affirmations are the key to getting started. Each morning, say to yourself, "I can do this and I will be successful". If you don't believe in yourself, why should anyone else?

Athletes never start a race with a losing frame of mind – they visualize their victory right from the beginning of the race and strive to achieve their vision.

Look at your vision board each time you feel down. Dream about your ideal job and your success. Remember, "you manifest your own reality".

CHAPTER 3

YOUR DECISION-MAKING PROCESS

Who is responsible?

Who do you think is responsible for your career? Your manager, the company? The organizational hierarchy?

It is easy to blame others, and it is a common fault in human beings. We shift the responsibility to others. Find excuses. There is always someone or something else to point the finger at.

But what role do you play in this whole scenario? Whose career is it you would like to change? Is it your career or that of others?

It is yours and no one else's. Once you are aware of this and have accepted that you are the only one who can change it, you can look at the next steps. Here are some questions for you to answer:

- Do you want to stay in the same organization? If yes, what is so great about your organization? What would happen if you did move somewhere else?

- If you do want to stay in the same organization, what do you want to see changing for you in your professional life? Is it your job title and role? If it is your title and role, what title would you aspire to and why?
- You want to stay at the same organization but to move to another department. Which section interests you the most and what is different there that you can't achieve in your current department?
- You want to move out of the organization. In this case, which industry or company attracts you the most and why? What does the new industry or organization offer that you don't have at your current one? What is so different? What do you expect to get from that move? What title or position are you looking for?
- Or you want to be your own boss. You want the pressure to be for your own purpose. What is so great about being your own boss? What do you expect? What is the business idea you have that you want to implement?

Once you know the answers to these questions, you can create your step-by-step action plan. However, you first need to go through this thinking process.

In all cases, you need to know yourself very well. In the appendices are some activities you can undertake, using a set of useful forms. These are helpful ways for you to assess your strong points. We don't look at the weaknesses, we look at your strengths and at ways to develop and focus your value proposition.

Activity 1: Be clear on your values

Using a series of exercises, you can list the values which are important to you, ending up with a 'Top 3' which should be your guide in all the decisions you make.

Activity 2: Evaluate your strengths

Here, there are a series of forms, listing skills you may possess in various areas:

- Communication
- Technology and IT
- Finance
- Supervision
- Management
- Teamwork
- Self-management
- Sales and marketing
- Physical and manual dexterity
- Other skills

Complete these forms openly and honestly, and you will see a picture emerging of where it is that your strengths lie. In the final 'Other skills' category, feel free to add any which have not been listed.

Another useful tool that you can use is the Wheel of Life, illustrated in Chapter 2, and included in the appendices at the end of the book.

In combination with your values, strengths and your personal model canvas, it's time to create your own value proposition and your mission statement. A great tool to help you to do this is to create your Personal Business Model Canvas, a one-page form where you can answer nine questions which will help you develop a clear plan for your future. Activity 6 in the Appendices gives you a blank Canvas form for you to complete. For the entrepreneurs out there, a variation on this is also available, the Business Model Canvas, and this is available for use in Activity 7.

So, in essence, who do you want to help and how, what are your skills and what is important to you, and what are your values?

What's next? Believe in yourself, your skills, your ability, your value to the company and, more importantly, to yourself. Whatever you decide, if you don't believe in yourself, no one else will.

Start your day with affirmations, as described in Chapter 1. Create a healthy relationship with yourself. That you are good enough, do enough and are capable enough. You are great as you are.

But of course, this is not sufficient.

Decide on your goals

Think about a time when you felt really happy in your job. What did you do? Which skills did you use? These should sit with your natural traits and since this made you happy, it was aligning with you as a person, your values, your mission, your "Why", your passion.

Do you want to have those same sensations every day? I would imagine that I would hear a resounding "yes".

So, let's go to work then.

Once your brand statement is clear and you feel it is resonating with you, find your own unique value proposition.

- What is it you offer your organization, any organizations, or yourself and others?
- What is your personal best as a peer/manager?
- How would you like to be perceived, firstly for yourself and then by others?

A great tool to use is your Personal Business Model Canvas, see the appendices, where you are exploring what you bring to the table, how you communicate, which resources you have and what you expect in return.

Focus on your mindset

Let's shift gears. It's all about the mindset. **If you don't believe in yourself, why should others?** I cannot overemphasise how important this is!

Improve your mindset using positive affirmations to yourself and to uncover your own misconceptions. You might need someone to help you with this, like a friend — someone you can trust completely who is non-judgemental and you can use to be open and bounce ideas off.

A coach is a great resource, someone external who has no preconceived opinions about you. Or you may choose to take on a mentor.

I hear you asking: what is the difference between these?

There are many differences between a coach and mentor. Let's explode the myth.

A mentor will share with you his/her own experiences and will give concrete guidance and directions, mainly someone who is in the same profession you want to move on in. A coach is an active listener but on top of this asks powerful, sometimes challenging questions to unleash your own potential from you in your own words. It is a results-orientated approach, a collaboration and an alliance where the coach is assisting you to shape the life you desire. A coach does not need to come from the same industry, company or profession. A coach is the expert in asking the questions you avoided, and empowers you to look into your deep self in a non judgemental and safe space.

Let's move on to consider what you can do yourself.

What exactly are your misconceptions? Here are some common examples:

- I am not good enough
- I don't know enough
- I can't do this
- This is too risky
- Who would hire me in different organizations?
- Who would do business with me?

And you might have more. Articulate these openly and with a loud voice, as whatever is said out loud sticks in your mind. Your subconscious mind will pull out everything associated with these words. All your emotions.

Let's undertake an exercise. Close your eyes, breathe in deeply on the count of 4 and exhale on the count of 4. Repeat this breathing exercise until you feel relaxed. Now, think about a scenario when you first had these emotions, who was with you and where it took place. Once you have visualized the past, create a mantra for yourself. Let go, release this core belief, and let your subconscious mind know that you now choose to do the opposite. Rewire your brain, your mind and your emotions. Let your passion come through. Imagine success, and the first steps towards it. Feel it, see it, hear it. You have the power over your brain. No one else does.

The importance of goal setting

This is very important. We might think we have all this in our head, but a goal without writing it down is not going to give you the results that you would wish for.

Whatever is written will get done. Create your SMART goals – everyone in the business world knows this acronym:

S – Specific
M – Measurable
A – Achievable
R – Relevant
T – Time-bound

And I like to add two more, to make them SMARTER:

E – Exciting
R – Results orientated

What is a goal if it is not exciting? Moreover, it must be challenging and that's why you have chosen to act.

Shoot for the stars. Yes, but eat your big elephant in chunks. Compartmentalize all your thoughts, wishes and hopes.

Think about the first step that needs to be taken to achieve your goal:

- By when are you going to do it?
- Who is going to hold you accountable?
- Who can support you?

Let's face it, we all need help, someone who can help us to follow up on our commitment to a goal and can make sure we are somehow kept on track. It's easy to procrastinate, especially when our subconscious mind is playing games with us to convince us, "Hey, you can't do this, stay where you are". Get that voice out of your head and say out loud, "I am stronger than you and I will do it whatever it takes!" It will not be an easy path, but it will be an amazing one. A new journey that will give you the fulfilment you are aiming for.

Your goal setting will be like a project plan, an implementation plan, like in your current job, where you need to plan for your team and for your own actions. Now, though, it is for yourself.

List all your goals step-by-step – tiny little steps set down using the SMARTER framework. Remember, each step counts and is a step forward to your own realization.

Once you have completed your first SMARTER goal, create the next one to be accomplished the week after.

Every little step is equally important.

Create your personal business plan

This is a really important step to help you to clarify exactly what you want to do and how you are going to achieve your purpose. So, what should be included in your business plan?

- **Create your elevator pitch:** This should be your strong, brief story. Rehearse it with friends, mentors and coaches. It should contain in brief, your personal information combined with some of your strengths plus one achievement, relevant to the audience.
- **Examine the industry/hierarchy/competition:** What skills are needed to move in that direction? And do you possess them? What mastery do you have of them? Good, very good, intermediate or zero.
- **How to upskill yourself:** If you don't have the necessary knowledge, this can be learned, so check if you need to upskill yourself. Might this require going on training outside the organization? If you know of a relevant training course provided by the company, ask to be put on it. Or if you need more insight information, contact the relevant stakeholders in the company/ industry to find out what is needed and how it works.
- **Research where you want to move to:** Read relevant articles/ newsletters about your organization or industry. Remember, knowledge is power.
- **The resources you need:** Check what other resources you need to move forward. This might require connecting with the right people, more reading, or networking inside or outside the organization.
- **How to raise your profile:** Start to participate in town-hall type meetings in your organization, or training webinars that are

offered by your company, or outside organization webinars in the area you want to move into. There is so much on offer, you just need to know where to look for it. Start by looking on LinkedIn, Meetup and other online resources.

As a rule of thumb: Be curious!

Be curious

Offer your services – offer to help – even if it means a bit more workload, specifically in areas or projects that you are interested in. This will all give you valuable experience. For example, offer job shadowing in the department you want to move to.

Be courageous

You have got nothing to lose. What is the worst that can happen? You have tried it and it didn't work. But you learned something new. Always look on the bright side.

Be positive

Having a positive mindset is half the battle won. There is nothing to fear. Always remind yourself about the mindset section. And if something did not work out as you wished for, which can and will happen, you have gained some experience which you can use for your next move, getting closer to your goal.

For entrepreneurs out there:

- Know what problem you are solving, what the pain points you would like to address or need addressing
- Conduct interviews with your target audience to understand their struggles and identify your target audience

- Create a prototype, which might be just as sketches or by offering pro bono services to test the waters and trial run your process
- Conduct a pulse check. Ask for feedback or, as I name it, feedforward, as this is information to move you one step ahead. This is also applicable for any business professional as an employee.

CHAPTER 4

GET OUT OF YOUR HAMSTER WHEEL

Have you made your decision?

After clarifying and shortlisting your values in the appendices in Activity 1, and conducting your skills/strengths assessment in Activity 2, what is the result?

Questions to ask yourself:

- Are you living your mission statement?
- How much, on a scale from 1-10 (10 being the highest), do you feel your values are being met?
- Your strengths – how much are you using them in your current job? Again, rate them on a scale from 1-10.
- How often do you feel frustrated during each day, week or month?
- How much does it bother you? Again, on a scale from 1-10?
- Do you feel recognized and appreciated by your peers and managers? Rate yourself.

Once you have responded to the questions above, and it turns out that you feel OK where you are, that's fine. You don't NEED to change. This is an exercise to assess yourself, take a moment to step back and look at your current job from a different perspective.

Do you feel deep down in your heart that it is time to change something?

Let's see what the next steps are. I have already encouraged you, in Chapter 3, to create your personal business plan, but let's now explore what else is needed.

Work smarter, not harder

Working smarter, not harder, means **having a clear strategy to prioritise your most important activities,** so you end each productive day feeling satisfied rather than overwhelmed, overcommitted, frustrated and overworked. Everyone may have their own definition of working smarter, not harder.

Work will never end, so to try to finish everything will never happen. Which of course is good as you need to have something to do the next day! However, you need to have addressed urgent client requests and those tasks that needed to be completed today, for example the report that had to be submitted by today's deadline. Then, beyond that, organize your day or your week so that you can set aside some time to read relevant newsletters and announcements from your organization or the industry that you want to move into. Keep absorbing new insights. For example, plan this activity once a week. Become more informed.

Remember, "Knowledge is power". Keep up to date with the strategies and the direction of your company or the company/industry you want to move into. If you aspire to be an entrepreneur, read books and articles, listen to podcasts, and watch webinars related to your desired sector.

You need to act – no one else can do this for you and that means finding time for all this activity and that needs to be planned wisely. I know you have plenty on your plate already, workwise and personally.

However, check which activities you can set aside or postpone, to create some time for your own self-development.

You can't do this alone either, so you need help.

Remember, you are the 'CEO' of your career, the Chief Empowerment Officer, and you empower yourself.

Create your Board of Directors

And a CEO never works alone. A CEO has a team looking after finance, administration, legal issues, sales and marketing etc. And so do you. You need people. So, you need to create your own 'Board of Directors'. Start by asking these questions to help to find the best candidates:

- How can your board of directors help you gain expertise, credibility and/or visibility?
- Who are your prospective board members?
- List each person's expertise.
- Who does each person know that you want to know?
- What are their professional and personal interests?
- What are their networks, memberships, hobbies, charitable organizations/causes?

In the appendices is Activity 3, following the steps to create your Board of Directors chart, and here is a visual of how the columns look on that chart.

List all the individuals that come to mind before you fill out any other columns. Then, after you finish brainstorming your list, analyse each individual, based on the subjects in the

Board of Directors list

Name of Prospective Member of Board of Directors	Area of Expertise	Type (Strategic, Operational, Developmental)	Role (Influencer, Connector)	What are his/her interests?	What do I have to offer?

columns to the right. Remember, you may not be able to complete every column for each individual and so you may need to collect more information to ascertain if the person will be valuable as a person on your personal board. And once you have established who can support, sponsor or vouch for you, you need to approach each candidate directly, in person or on the phone. Just writing to them is not sufficient, as it will not be seen as a sufficiently serious request.

So how do we approach this? Remember your elevator pitch. Yes, you need to introduce yourself somehow. Depending on your relationship with the person you listed, you need to mention who you are, what you do and your reason for choosing to reach out to them.

A first step is to know how to promote yourself. As human beings, we are not always good at this. All too often we just make the assumption, "Hey, my manager knows what I am doing and what I am capable of" but, remember, they won't know every detail or necessarily be clear on what you would like to do, what your goals are, or where your passion or your interest lies. The same applies if you want to be an entrepreneur. You need to articulate all this, clearly, consistently, and regularly.

Use the STAR model

Firstly, right now, how do you promote yourself and your accomplishments? Do you even do this at all?

Either way, you need to start, and here is a useful model which is an objective way to frame what you bring to the table. It is the STAR model.

S – Situation: Describe a scene, the who, what, when of a situation you have been in.

T – Task: Talk about the objective, issue or obstacle that you had to address.

A – Action: Talk about your role in this scenario, what action you took as opposed to that taken by your team. Refer to the team of course but make sure you mention yourself, including the 'I statement'. For example: "I organized a meeting with my team to discuss how we can resolve the issue and we undertook a brainstorm. Afterwards, I distributed relevant agreed tasks to each team member, and I coordinated all the actions taken".

R – Results: Outline the results of your actions. Include the impact that you had on the situation and that your team had.

You can use this model in any situation – for your performance reviews, meetings with your manager or any other peer, or with senior managers. It is objective, results orientated and reflects what you bring to the table as you, your authentic self.

Make sure you have some examples ready to talk about if you find the opportunity to do so. Not just one but a selection of them to suit the person you are talking to and its relevance to the moment you are in. I am sure you have various success stories to draw from.

Create a success journal

Another important tip: create and update a success journal. This can be simply in a scrapbook, or on Excel, Word, Evernote or whichever tool is good for you. To ensure you keep it updated, just make each journal entry short and quick. Each entry will help you to reflect on what you have delivered and are still delivering to your company with your skills and abilities. We tend to forget what we have done throughout the year. A success journal will show you in written format what you have achieved.

And you can use this information in any scenario, discussion or negotiation with your audience.

It is also a good reminder on how successful and productive you are and what impact you have on the business.

We don't fully realise this until we write these things down. If writing is not your thing, then use your imagination – you can record your voice or create a short video collection for yourself.

Create your elevator pitch

Now we can move to our elevator pitch framework.

1. Tell me about you in two sentences
2. Name your three greatest strengths in six words or less
3. Name your two most significant accomplishments in or outside your organization

As CEO, commit to yourself to feel comfortable and confident in being able to answer all these easily. These will ultimately help when promoting you and your message and will be invaluable when you are out networking.

When we think about our purpose, goals and strengths, it is important to reflect on what we know and want.

It's time to go networking

We are now entering exciting territory. It is time to go networking.

No one can advance alone in their professional life.

You have now established the list of your Board of Directors. Let's deep dive a bit more into your network.

We have 3 types of networks of people:

1. Strategic

- They see trends unfolding in your organization and the external business environment.
- They are located in various functions, business units, and levels within your organization.
- They may also work outside your organization.

2. Operational

- This is the team you work with to accomplish your everyday work – your peers, direct reports, and superiors in the organization.
- There may also be key outsiders, such as various external stakeholders and partners to the company.

3. Developmental

- These may be other managers and other people within your organization who you respect and admire and who you can learn from.
- There may also be colleagues from previous jobs, members of professional associations, alumni groups, clubs, and your circles of friends and acquaintances. They all possess different experiences which can help your development.

What is the benefit of networking and why should we do it? Especially as it can seem frightening at times, and you may not feel confident in launching yourself into networking with others.

"Networking is the number 1 unwritten rule for success" – Sallie Krawcheck, sometimes referred to as the most powerful woman on Wall Street.

- Gain insights – gather insider information
- Gain knowledge
- Find out early about new opportunities
- Find mentors and sponsors
- Create visibility
- Gain new connections

- Learn and become inspired
- Develop interpersonal relationships
- Create your brand and build your image
- People start to get to know you
- Give and receive referrals
- Help others

By spreading your message in this way, you will be remembered as and when any opportunity arises within your network. This is why networking is essential and such an important part of developing your professional career.

Below you will see the networking wheel. Here is how to use this in targeting your networking. You can find a blank version for you to complete yourself in the appendix Activity 8.

Here are the instructions:

1. Since you will probably want to analyze several different networks, give this network a name on the following page (eg "Developmental network"; "Project X network")

2. Describe the network's purpose. For example, is the network aimed at helping you accomplish a specific business task, complete an important project, or enhance your professional growth?

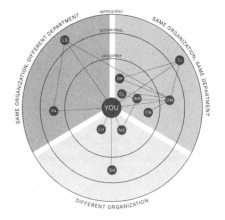

3. List the names of the individuals who are currently members of the network.

4. Map the members listed in your table onto the blank circular diagram: Consider yourself as the centre of the network. Position each member of your network on the map, labelling them with the initials of their names:

- Use the rings around the centre to position your network members according to how frequently you interact with them:
  - » Frequently (eg at least weekly)
  - » Occasionally (eg monthly)
  - » Infrequently (eg less than monthly)
- Position the members on the relevant section of the diagram:
  - » Same organization and same department as you
  - » Same organization but different department than you
  - » Different organization than you
- Draw lines connecting you to the members of the network whom you have direct contact with.
- Draw lines connecting members of your network if the members know one another. If you anticipate having many lines, it may be helpful to use a different colour or a dotted line for these connections.

Ultimately, the networking wheel is a way to check who-knows-who in your network and how you can best reach out to someone who you don't know but your close contact knows. It shows you at the centre, and then concentric circles of influence spreading out. It is an excellent visual representation of how diverse your network should be.

Remember what I mentioned earlier on: Work smarter, not harder. One way to do this is to set time aside for networking and not to focus solely on working. Yes, it requires time and effort, and of course, it is still work. The clue is in its name: Net-WORK.

You have examined your network and you can see who can be useful for your needs.

Here now comes the question: how will you reach out? Face-to-face or virtually? How to start conversations inside or outside your organization?

Let's split this into three different types of networking: Frequent – Occasional – Infrequent. These sections are in your network wheel.

Frequent: This is probably the easiest one to get started and to sustain, especially if your contacts are within your organization. The simplest way is to contact them directly. Even if you don't have any relationship with them, they will at least know of your position in the organization and you are, in turn, able to identify that person's role in the business. Ask for a coffee chat, either over Zoom or preferably face-to-face, in the cafeteria or outside. Trust me, to 99% of these types of requests you will receive a "Yes". Don't overthink what to say or how to start. Go with the flow a bit. You can give some broad context for the chat such as:

"We have never had the opportunity to have a chat and so I thought it would be good to share a coffee. Also, I know you are working on XYZ project, which sounds very interesting, and I would like to know more…"

This is just one example. You can create your own, depending on whether you know the person or not, but the important thing is to ask for an opening connection, regardless of what you expect from this first meeting. Is it a promotion you are after, or do you know that a new position will soon be available? Or, as in my example, you simply want to be part of a new project.

Just set it up and see what comes out. If you don't articulate your wishes how will anyone know what you would like to do? No one knows what you want if you don't communicate it.

And make sure this is not a one-way process. Networking is not just about trying to get as much as you can from your network. You need to be generous with your time, share YOUR connections, and offer your expertise, your services and your skills. The person you contact also has some goals to achieve, so help them to succeed, with your energy, your experience and your knowledge.

Occasional: Examine who, from your close contacts, knows this person that you think would be beneficial for you. Ask your direct contact how you can reach them, ask for a short intro email, coffee chat or virtual Zoom meeting and reach out. The same principle applies as in the Frequent section in how to start a conversation and continue.

Infrequent: This type of networking is a bit trickier... but not impossible. See who knows this important person for you to advance in your professional life: it can be from your close circle or from the Occasional bucket. It is again up to you to reach out via your own closer contacts.

Imagine that this is a dance, and you live in the moment. You can't predict what the other person will say. Whatever they say, don't take it personally. It might be a positive or a not-so-positive response, but either way it is a connection where you took the initiative, and that shows leadership and a proactive attitude. Go with the flow. Like in a dance, go with the conversation. You will learn so much and, remember, it is important to share from your side too.

What you can do is be prepared with your success stories, your elevator pitch, your passion. Be sure to show it!

Rest assured, by using all these tools you will stay in the head of the connected person. And then, once an opportunity arises, they will reach out to you.

You are planting the seeds now. Which one will bloom and will bear fruit, who knows?? But you can be sure that one will produce fruit, and then this will be your time.

CHAPTER 5

OTHER MEANS OF EXPOSURE

We have established our network, created our success journal, and developed our elevator pitch and our brand statement.

Great! What else can we do to position ourselves in a new or existing industry and in our current position?

Use LinkedIn.

Social media is of course now the most widespread tool used for networking and exposure. However, for our purposes here, we are not talking about Instagram or Facebook, but the social media platform which is focused on our professional life – LinkedIn.

LinkedIn is not just a recruitment or job search social media platform. It is so much more than that. It is the platform for creating your professional social media brand. The more you post the more you will be seen and recognised as an expert in your field.

If you are employed by a company, in the past you might have hesitated to be active on LinkedIn, as the perception perhaps would be that your managers would think that you are actively looking for another job. However, this is not the case anymore. With your posts, you create trustworthiness for your company and for yourself. People will reach out to you proactively to be connected. They may ask you to be a guest speaker, ask for your advice or even start a conversation to know more about you and your interests, or offer their services.

Whether you actively participate in your career or not, someone will create your brand, if you are not taking charge. Better to act yourself to create your own one on social media.

Your LinkedIn profile is your business card. Wherever you go networking the easiest way to share your contact info is use this technology to your advantage. It is really easy to create a digital business card, stored on your phone. There are many different apps available for creating these, just search app stores for 'Digital business card'. Using these, you can share not just basic contact info, but also your bio, CV and all your social media links. This can be shared phone-to-phone, be used as your email signature or on social media.

Let's get back to LinkedIn.

Your LinkedIn profile should be fully completed and speak about you, your interests, your passions and what you do.

Here are some guidelines to follow to create a LinkedIn profile which maximises your ability to connect with people:

I. **Photo:** wear a nice shirt, specifically for men, or blouse/jumper. A jacket, and certainly a tie is no longer essential, but whatever you choose should reflect your personal style and how you like to be seen in your professional life. Face the camera and look friendly, with a nice smile, although not too exaggerated. For the background, either plain white or grey, or a general office atmosphere but not with flowers or anything that will distract from looking at your face. If you are a branding and marketing person, a bit more creativity might be relevant. Don't just take a selfie! In fact, this photo is so important it is worth investing in one from a professional photographer who can ensure the lighting and the background are perfect. For inspiration, you can check my profile at: https://www.linkedin.com/in/hulyakurt-innkick/

2. **LinkedIn banner:** Don't use the default LinkedIn banner. Change it to one that reflects the branding of your company or your profession. For example, if you are a trader, choose a picture which reflects a trading floor. Or, if you deal with data and analysis, choose a picture with a chart. You can create your own banner using pictures from a free platform such as Canva.com. They have pre-prepared banners you can customise.

3. **Your tagline:** Don't just use your job title. Add more about what you do, explain in a nutshell what you provide, who you can help and how. Here you can use elements of your elevator pitch. Again, for inspiration, check out mine. You have 120 characters to play with and you can use some emojis in-between as well. Be aware that emojis use more than one character. Use keywords relevant to your industry. People using LinkedIn's search engine optimizer will look for specific keywords and from these you might be headhunted or receive connections proactively. The aim is to apply the pull rather than the push method.

4. **About Me:** Don't merely copy your CV. Anyone who is interested in your profile will only see the first 2-3 sentences, so the opening part is crucial. Tell people about your passion – start with what you like and love to do and continue with a brief history/summary. People love stories. Think about how you can relay your story to your family or kids. Use clear and simple language.

5. **Recommendations:** These are important, and people will be checking from whom you have received recommendations. Ask for some if you don't have any. Specifically, from either your managers, peers, or anyone you have worked for. These are testimonials which reinforce your credibility. Don't ask for recommendations from someone who is not related to what you do or aspire to do.

6. **Features and pictures:** Make sure to have some media uploaded, like pictures from a conference you have attended or the flyer

which featured you presenting your company. Remember, people love photos and images, now more than ever.

7. **Certificates:** Upload relevant diplomas and certificates.
8. **Work history:** Pick up your current company's logo from the drop-down in LinkedIn when you create your work history.

These are some basic tips to create an attractive LinkedIn profile. Remember, this will be your business card, or could be your gateway to a new job, to a successful entrepreneurship or to a new position in a company.

Once all this is done, visibility does not just come from a great profile. You need to be active on LinkedIn. How?

By sharing articles, by posting what you do, attending a specific conference, adding to your learnings.

When sharing articles, don't simply share the article but add your brief opinion about it too. Or ask a question, maybe even be controversial. Grab the attention of the audience by engaging and commenting. Tag specific people or hashtag your industry and company. For example, these are the sorts of hashtags I use for my coaching: #coachingwithhulya #lifecoaching #businesscoaching #noblemanhattan.

Another easy way to maintain and be active is to make use of the notifications LinkedIn sends you. Check the notifications tab on your profile and you will see who has got a work anniversary or birthday. Don't think, hey this is not Facebook, we are professionals here. Yes, we are, but we are human as well and we like to be remembered and recognised. Don't just use the pre-worded blurb from LinkedIn but add your 5 cents to it. What I do is that I leave the pre-worded LinkedIn wording and add "Wishing you a great special day". Also, when you see an interesting post and think, hey this is great, not only like it but put a comment in. Ensure these are your genuine thoughts and what comes from your heart. Of course, conduct due diligence by not offending people or using poor phrasing. Be professional yet ensure that this comes across as something clearly directly from you.

All these actions will create visibility and credibility.

Anyone you would like to connect with, send them a direct message. Believe me, most people will respond positively if you reach out in the correct way. And if they don't respond, don't take it personally!

Where else can we create visibility?

A great place, particularly following the huge growth in popularity since the pandemic, is during Zoom meetings. If it is not a Zoom webinar, you can send direct messages via the Chat facility. If it is a Zoom webinar, you don't have the Chat option available, so, anyone who impresses you, make a note of their name and then connect over LinkedIn, with a personal note.

And make sure your Zoom background, either a virtual one, or in-the-room with a banner behind you, reflects your branding and your image! Or use LinkedIn in conjunction with Zoom by sending a personal LinkedIn message after or even during your Zoom call, saying, "Dear xyz, We have been on the same Zoom call. I was interested in what you were saying about... and I would love to stay connected."

Whether you are in the office or work from home, during your team meetings ensure that your voice is heard. Make a comment, provide feedback, ask for clarification if you don't understand, add to someone's suggestion. Your opinion matters. Remember, every input counts and your opinion is as valid as anyone else's. This shows that you are engaged, and it will be noticed by your managers and peers. Sometimes, you might even touch on a point that is sensitive, or everyone has got it on their mind but are reluctant to speak out. Be the first to comment!

And for that, you need to have an assertive communication style. What are the characteristics of such a style? Some are listed here:

1. **Direct eye contact:** This shows that the speaker is strong and not intimidated. Even on Zoom.
2. **An assertive stance or posture:** However, this must be with the right balance of strength and casualness. For example, standing rigid may come across as aggressive, whereas slouching may be perceived as weak. Again, this also applies on Zoom.
3. **Tone of voice:** A strong voice conveys assertiveness but raising one's voice shows aggression and is likely to be met with anger.
4. **Facial expression:** Expressions that are neither angry nor anxious are essential for sending the right message.
5. **Timing:** Assertive communication must be executed at the right time (eg not cutting across your manager in a public Zoom meeting when they are making a point)
6. **Non-threatening, non-blaming language:** For example, language such as *"If you continue to do that, you will be sorry!"* is threatening rather than assertive.
7. **Clarity:** For example, *"Can you please not be that way?"* is vague, while *"Can you please not walk away when we're talking?"* more clearly conveys the speaker's needs.
8. **Positive language:** For example, making a negative request such as *"Will you stop leaving your papers all over the house?"* is less effective than a positive request: *"Here is a divider I've set up. Will you please place your papers here?"*
9. **Language without criticism of oneself or others:** For example, phrases such as *"I know I'm overly sensitive, but could you please not use that word?"* and, *"Didn't anyone ever teach you any manners?"* are critical rather than assertive.

How can you put all this into practice? You need to try things out and a good place to start is to test things on your friends. They will soon let you know if your tone and style is appropriate, but in a way that doesn't have the same consequences as testing things out on your manager! You might already have an assertive style, and that is great, but for the ones who don't, practice makes perfect.

The importance of feedforward

Whatever your situation, ask for feedback or, as I call it, "Feedforward". Why feedforward? Because it will give you input to move you ahead, to improve. The more you dare to ask, the more you will be even more effective. It is difficult to ask for, as we are afraid of criticism. This information is not personal though; this is for your own good. We all have blind spots as we are too close to our own job, therefore it is so important to get other people's opinions to show you what you may have failed to mention or do. This information is so precious. And you can get feedforward not only from your peers but also from your family and your friends. At times, this can be even better as they don't know the context, and on that basis may ask questions that make you think, "Wow I never thought about that".

Body language

Be aware that your body language and your voice play a huge role in your ability to emphasise your point, statement, suggestion or comment. Even if you are on Zoom, sit straight, with both feet on the ground and arms on the chair or on the table. Be well dressed and don't slouch. Look into the camera, remember to have your camera on (!) and don't be on mute when you are trying to speak!

Tone of voice

Your voice is your instrument. Speak loud and clear and remember that it may well be likely that not everyone is native English or whatever your language is. Inject some variety into your pace and pitch. Sometimes use a higher and sometimes lower voice tone. Use pauses, as these can be very powerful, as people wait to hear what you next have to say.

It is not about what you say, it is about how you say it.

Use the sandwich method

Have you heard about the sandwich method of delivering an opinion?

Imagine you have the first layer of the sandwich, which is a tasty, fresh slice of bread. You then have your cheese + ham filling, and then you have another slice of bread.

How to interpret that into a comment? Well, your first slice of bread is a positive comment, your filling is your feedforward and your second slice of bread is a further positive comment. For example:

"I appreciate your helpful comments about xyz and I really think this is crucial, but it would be even more effective if we could add this suggestion of mine... In this way, we'll all be helping our team goals."

So, at any given time, you can use the sandwich method. If you are a manager and you need to give input relating to performance. Or you want to give feedforward to your manager.

Also, you can give your opinion or suggestion in an email. For example:

"That was a great meeting today, and from it I did some brainstorming, and I came up with some ideas to improve our process to achieve excellent customer satisfaction.

Please allow me to add this idea...

I'm sure you'll be able to develop this further, so I look forward to your feedback..."

Summary

In essence, you can create your brand and develop your image both outside and inside your organization by being proactive. It is all about adopting the mindset shift that only you are responsible for this, and you can do even more than I have listed, as you are the subject-matter expert in your organization, field and industry. You know it all!

You just need to apply it! From nothing comes nothing.

All these tasks may seem to be a bit overwhelming but if you split them into little goals using SMARTER, you will see how you can reach them one by one. **Determination is key to success.**

And all this might be only one small part of your bigger goal. That's fine as well. **The important thing is to take action!**

CHAPTER 6

CONTINUOUS LEARNING AND IMPROVEMENT

We have talked about your social media presence, specifically LinkedIn for professionals. And about your presence during webinars and online meetings.

These tips are the same for face-to-face meetings too. Whenever you are in a face-to-face, make sure to be present, in the form of asking a question or making a comment and adding to anyone's ideas.

Don't censor yourself too much, just go for it. If you know the subject being addressed already, you can prepare a bit beforehand as to what to say or what ideas you may bring to the table.

If you are someone trying to move out of your current organization or you are planning to become an entrepreneur, search for connections in the industry you are looking for. You have done your networking wheel, right? Check who can support you, out of those you are in contact with. And just reach out!

Look around you

What does this mean? Rather than cracking on just with working, you need to know what's going on in either the industry you want to move into or within your organization or as an entrepreneur. For that, read any newsletters and articles that are relevant.

I know, from my previous corporate experience, that people say, "I don't have time for that – I have work to do!" Yes, of course you have work to do, everyone does. But if it is not super urgent, ie anything which impacts customer service severely, try to set some time aside to read, listen and make connections.

An example: we always had townhall-style face-to-face meetings on a quarterly basis and usually we had senior managers present. Meaning not only managers based locally but also senior managers from abroad who were visiting our Geneva office. I always made the time to be there. Why? As it was important to hear about what's going on. Yes, this might sound a bit boring but in amongst this would also be insights on trends, the vision of the company and upcoming significant projects. By attending these meetings, you can just go over to the presenter afterwards and introduce yourself and ask some questions. You can show your interest by saying, "I would like to be part of this" or you can simply show your appreciation and thank them for the great presentation. This could prove to be a great way to make contact with senior people. And you will stick in their minds. If anything relevant comes up, they might remember you more easily and might reach out to you at the point of developing a new opportunity.

Step forward and volunteer

Another nice move is to raise your hand to volunteer for a project, or an initiative the company has. This will mean a bit more work, but it will give you exposure and the opportunity to work with other peers and project managers.

In such situations it can become more apparent that you have plenty to offer apart from your day-to-day experience, and you can mention this as an example of going above and beyond during your performance review, to help you to ask for a promotion or a pay rise. However, volunteer activity should also be conducted in just such a spirit, as you are primarily volunteering to help and to give something back, not just to improve your pay!

If you are interested in volunteering outside your organization, check out what volunteer or interest groups are out there. Subscribe, become a member and but be an active one. In any volunteer organization, active members are always in short supply. Being proactive is always important.

I am in a volunteer organization, an NGO, a non-profit, supporting women in trade and business: OWIT – Organization of Women in International Trade. I know what it takes to run it. I spend some time outside my work setting to discuss strategy, plans, organize events, make sure the team is aligned, motivate them and have people who can take accountability. We need to trust each other, we delegate, pass on activities and everyone steps in to move things forward. Yes, you get frustrated sometimes and ask yourself why you are doing this, and I have done this too. But it is thanks to my volunteer activities that I have increased my network exponentially. Has that helped me to advance in my endeavours? Of course it has! I can now reach out to so many people to get advice, to feedforward, receive opportunities to be a speaker and find offers and referrals.

Remember, people do business with people. And they trust their best friends' or peers' advice. Just like you would do. Put yourself in the shoes of the hiring manager or the people you want to do business with. Who would you trust?

Coming back to volunteering:

Firstly, only become a volunteer member in a cause you believe in, or you will not sustain your interest in it. It can, of course, be extremely helpful if it will give you new contacts, expand your network and that you will learn something.

Once you have decided on the group to be part of and you understand the dynamics, attend workshops as much as you can. Any face-to-face ones, after-work events. Yes, this requires time, but you will find that it is worth it, as you do it for your own fulfilment, and to get out of your little bubble. It is easy to sit on the sofa after work and just watch TV or Netflix. It requires grit to continue your path, like an athlete.

You need grit

Let's expand on grit, what is it?

Top athletes rely on grit, which really means mental strength. Grit helps you to focus, pay attention and persevere with something, even when something is distracting you, or it is boring, difficult, exhausting or challenging. The training regime of Olympic athletes is a good example of this: none of them would be able to endure their relentless training schedules without possessing grit. Studies of Olympic athletes, world class musicians and chess grand masters find that what they have in common is the ability to motivate themselves throughout their intense training routines.

You need to practise achieving grit; it is like weightlifting for the brain. The more you do it, the more you will gain the necessary muscles.

One of the techniques I would like to share as a coach is 'Athlete's Breath':

Breathe in deeply through the nostrils all the qualities of a top athlete – these qualities include focus, attention, strength, and grit. Then exhale slowly, allowing these qualities to settle deep inside you. As you do this, shift your position to represent a grittier attitude to life and to your work.

Work the workshop

After this deviation into grit, let's go back to our main subject. Take the time and make the extra effort for you to move to another niche, add to your experience toolkit and take another step forward to your goal.

During either F2F or online workshops, after work, you need again to be proactive. Anyone you can spot as someone that you would like to network with, as they fit your target industry or have a similar job that you want to move into, get in contact. Either via LinkedIn or direct message during the workshop. And don't just send a connection request, but ask them for a quick coffee chat, as you want to know more about a specific topic that they are involved in. Always end such connections with a call to action.

As we mentioned in the Grit section, you need to consistently repeat your networking, and your volunteering efforts. Some may not be particularly productive or useful, but some will be. Think about your board of directors – you might find connections or opportunities through your consistent approach. Someone knows someone who can help you. Even within your organization.

What you are doing now is planting the seeds and we don't know which one will grow into good fruit or vegetables.

1. Be courageous
2. Embrace change
3. Be optimistic
4. Celebrate failure

Number 4 may seem surprising, as it has a negative spin of course. But this is the only way you can progress, learn, grow, and succeed.

You need to try, otherwise you don't know if something is going to work or not.

In the innovation space, I always say, "Try fast, fail fast and learn fast". Let's face it, not every move and contact will give you the desired results but at least you will have tried.

Never Give Up is the motto.

Trust in the universe or destiny or whatever it is that you believe in or have faith in.

Moreover, one door leads to another and if you don't try, it will never open.

The treasure is inside you

A short motivational story to share with you:

"A beggar who was sitting on a box was always stopping people to ask for some money. One time a man passed by this beggar and as usual the beggar asked for money. This man said, "I don't have any myself so I can't give you anything". The beggar insisted a bit and the man said, "You are sitting on a box, have you checked what is in it?" and beggar said, "There is nothing inside – I know, as I have been sitting on it for years". The man insisted: "Have you ever opened it, have your tried to look inside?" The beggar said, "No, I never opened this box, it is an empty box, I am sure". "The man said, "Let's try together and open the box – let's see what is inside". The beggar turned the box upside down and they started to open the box together. Guess what was inside the box? It was filled with gold. A real treasure.

What is the essence of this anecdote?

You have all the power, the treasure inside you, you just need to find it. Sometimes you need a guide as the beggar had to have. Someone who challenges you, asks you the difficult questions. But the answers are with you, not with anyone else.

Seek help

So, don't hesitate to ask for help, which could be from peers, friends or family. Take on a mentor at your workplace or in the industry you want to move into. Believe me, people are ready to help, you just need to ask. And if someone declines to help, it will be because they are too busy and cannot give you the time you deserve. It will not be because they don't like you. So don't take it personally at all.

Another option is to work with a business coach, who would be asking all these powerful questions, trying to find the treasure within yourself, like in the beggar story, and create an action plan with you. Coaching is results driven. A coach will make you accountable. Also, a coach is non-judgemental, and will not give you direct advice and guidance. Instead, you will find it for yourself with the guidance of a coach.

As we mentioned earlier, a mentor is experienced in a specific field, profession or industry, and would be someone you can ask advice from, and this person would be providing his/her own experience. A mentor would be more directional whereas a coach would be asking open and challenging questions to encourage you to find the answers for yourself.

Depending on your needs, you might have a mentor and coach at same time as they would complement each other. Or you can choose to just have one or the other.

It is important that you have enough people around you, on your board of directors, who will support you, give you feedforward, advice and guidance.

You can't succeed on your own. There is always a team behind any successful person, in the form of work colleagues, professional advisers, family, or friends.

Sometimes you need to delegate, wait for answers, or let go.

It can be no bad thing to let go and try something else.

We like to blame ourselves, but don't. Adopt a way of thinking that we have mentioned: **Try fast, fail fast and learn fast.**

Having an agile and flexible mindset is imperative. Don't get stuck on one idea. It may be that your starting point turns out to not really be ideal or realistic. If you feel and sense that, pivot your action immediately and spend your energy on something else.

Take this as a learning curve and celebrate each step as you are on the journey to a more fulfilled professional life.

CHAPTER 7

GETTING INTO THE ROUTINE

Now you know that everything lies within yourself, and it is your responsibility, how can you maintain motivation and consistency and repeat your efforts in networking, self-promotion, constant learning and performing for your own brand?

What are the secret ingredients to relentlessly continuing, even if you don't see any quick results?

You are planting seeds; you need to leave time for the seeds to grow and flourish. Although you might give the same care to each of the seeds equally, some will flourish earlier than others or some will just die.

You might ask: OK, so why do I need to spend my precious time on seeds that will die?

Simple: you don't know which ones will fail! So, you need to keep on trying. From each seed you will learn something or get to know someone. Your efforts might seem to be for nothing and a waste of time. Believe me, they are not. You never know when these connections or knowledge will be useful to you.

I have a quote I would like to share: "From determination comes success".

You will lose belief in yourself and feel down. This is normal and you need to embrace the moments when you feel like this. In those moments, do something which will cheer you up. That could be different for everyone. Having a coffee with a friend, go for a walk or some other form of exercise – whatever is good for you, just have a short break. Give a pause to your brain and recharge your environment by doing something else.

During your brain pause, suddenly a new idea will come your way, or your friend will trigger a new idea by making a comment.

Our brain is interesting.

What often happens to me is that my best ideas come during taking a shower or walking around or right before I am closing my eyes. This pause gives you fresh inspiration.

If that happens to you, hold that thought and try to write it down as soon as possible. When you are in bed just raise yourself and write it down so it is off your head and down on paper, otherwise you will forget it or not be able to get back to sleep.

If you take a break, don't make it too long. It can be for 2-3 days but then just get back on course and on track. Otherwise, we go into the loop of losing our routine.

Reflect on potential obstacles:

What might be yours along your way that you need to overcome? Think about them and write them down:

1. _____

2. _____

3. _____

Adopt a growth mindset

What are the practical steps/plans you can make to maintain your growth mindset and continue to network, be alert, speak up, be engaged and look outside your working box?

Let's delve into 'growth mindset'. We are always talking about it but what does this mean in detail:

1. Passion for learning
2. Self-belief
3. Calculated risks
4. Living in the moment
5. Action counts
6. Accept exciting challenges
7. Self-discipline
8. Be surrounded by positivity
9. Helping others
10. Greater resilience

Let's explore each of these topics a bit more.

1. Passion for learning

People with a growth mindset have a desire to keep learning. Your goal is to improve your knowledge as much as possible, in the field or industry you would like to move into.

2. Self-belief

Belief in oneself is a fundamental quality. The truth is that people with a growth mindset have true belief in themselves. Whenever they encounter problems or challenges, they have a belief that they will overcome them. Once they overcome these challenges or setbacks, they will understand why they were there. This will help them improve their learning and experience. Your belief and your belief in yourself will help you move on.

"If you hear a voice inside you that says you can't paint, then paint, and that voice will be silenced." – Vincent van Gogh

3. Calculated risks

The difference between a steadfast mindset and a growth mindset is knowing how to take risks. The risk-reward scenario is a big determinant. People prepared to take calculated risks don't see themselves better placed if they have never taken a chance. Instead, they believe that it is better to take risks while accepting the risk of failure.

4. Live in the moment

Those with a growth mindset believe in living in the here and now. The past is the past and nothing can be done about it. Hence, people with a growth mindset have the ability to learn and grow. Focus on the present and don't worry or think about what might have happened.

They realize that this present moment is there for living, and it is here that a growth mentality creates a belief that they feel they can achieve something and grow. Also, they feel the past must be left as the past. There are those who are inhibited and those who, instead, dust themselves off and move forward again. Living in the present is an important growth quality.

5. Action counts

People who perform at their best are those who start small even though they dream big. They understand that they need a starting point, but from there they can take action. In acting and doing, the point is that they use their growth mentality to strengthen their awareness.

By taking action, they can apply their knowledge and it is this conscious practice that makes them successful. In life one has to act, of course, and acting can begin at any time in life. There are those who start this process in high school and those who do it in old age, but the main factor that supports this quality is that they step out from their comfort zone.

6. Accept exciting challenges

For those with a growth mindset, a challenge is something they embrace. In reality, they see a challenge as an opportunity to prove yourself. When such an opportunity comes up, they rise to the challenge and show that mindset enables people to succeed.

This makes them stronger and smarter. Sometimes challenges can be scary, but until you have faced that challenge, you may not know how you will react. People with a growth mindset believe that they can overcome any challenge they face and emerge from it as better people.

7. Self-disciplined

People with a growth mindset have a different thought process than others. When it comes to being successful and getting what they want, they are aware that they must work on it to achieve it. They have a great degree of self-discipline. This commitment allows them to focus fully on their ultimate goal. As a result, their rigorous efforts and determination enable them to succeed and get to where they want to be. They don't waste time proving they can, they go beyond their basic skills and find a path to success with a positive attitude.

8. Surrounded by positivity

People with a growth mindset are optimistic and this is one of those solid traits that comes with being a highly effective individual. Of course, they experience challenging and difficult times in life, but their positivity enables them to form stronger new attitudes through which they understand the meaning of positivity. Positivity is something that leads to success. A growth mentality is what you need to move forward and achieve.

9. Helping others

Successful people are fully aware of the importance of helping others. Everyone needs someone's help at some point in their life and this helps them to understand how important it is to help others. Here they realise that skills can be developed with a little guidance and help. What supports this mindset is that if you want to get what you want, you need to help others. Hence, your goal is to help people every day, as this often results in you receiving more than you have invested.

10. Greater resilience

Resilience is one of the key qualities of the growth mindset. Growth is not something that happens in the blink of an eye. It doesn't happen overnight. Highly effective people know that success is not easy. This means that they are committed as much as possible to achieving their goals.

This is regardless of whether they are always on track all the time. They'll keep going until they come out the other side. In this way they can continue on their path to growth and success. People with a growth mindset accept failure as a means of learning and improvement. They think that challenges help them grow, and that effort and persistence will help them to prevail.

Shift your mindset, and to do this, you need to keep repeating the same behaviour. For that you need to be conscious of your actions, be aware and find an anchor or a trigger that will remind you to act in this shifted mindset way rather than staying in your comfort zone.

How can we set an anchor in our mind? What is an anchor in the first place?

Wikipedia tells us that an anchor is a device, normally made of metal, used to secure a vessel to the bed of a body of water to prevent the craft from drifting due to wind or current. The word derives from Latin ancora, which itself comes from the Greek ἄγκυρα. Anchors can either be temporary or permanent.

Now let's explore the meaning in the NLP world, Neuro Linguistic Programming:

In NLP, 'anchoring' refers to **the process of associating an internal response with some external or internal trigger** so that the response may be quickly, and sometimes covertly, re-accessed.

A quick and practical tip to set an anchor:

Be the person you want to be: anytime, anywhere.

Decide what feeling you would like to access with an anchor, then:

1. Remember a time when you felt totally: (the feeling)

2. As you step back into that time, see again everything that was going on around you, and hear again whatever sounds you could hear around you, and re-experience that feeling of total (the feeling)

3. As that feeling builds to a peak, set the anchor by pressing on a knuckle or pressing a thumb and finger together for a few seconds, then release.

4. Break that mental state by thinking about something completely different.

5. Repeat the process from step 1), using the same memory and the same anchor spot twice more.

6. When the anchor has been set 3 times, test it by pressing the anchor spot.

7. Notice the result. You will know you have got it right when you experience the feeling without having to re-access the memory to which it was associated.

Source: NLP – *Elegant Coaching*, Noble Manhattan Coaching

Once you have set an anchor it is important that you remember your anchor and use it as often as you can. The more you practise, the more it becomes a behaviour.

Think of it like starting to learn to drive a car. In the beginning, you are very conscious, making sure you check the gears, brakes, side lights and mirrors. After you get used to driving, you don't even pay attention to any of these anymore. The same is applicable for acquiring new behaviours, new ways of remembering and have these embedded in your day-to-day routine without even thinking of it.

Summary

Think about these aspects as part of creating your new routine which will help you get off the hamster wheel:

- Determination
- Focus
- Identify and overcome potential obstacles
- Adopt a growth mindset
- Explore practical tips for anchoring, using NLP techniques.

Food for thought

- What small thing are you going to do?
- When and how are you going to do it?
- Who and what can help you to achieve it?
- What could get in your way?
- How are you going to overcome that obstacle?
- What is the level of your commitment?
- How much do you believe that you are going to do what you say?

Don't just think about these but write them down! Whatever is written, gets done and sticks in your mind.

It's important and a step forward to your goals to either handwrite them, make bullet points or use any application or software to hold your thoughts. The human mind forgets quickly so make sure you have it recorded somewhere.

CHAPTER 8

FEAR AND ANXIETY

Fear is the one of the strongest emotions. It has a very powerful impact on your body and mind.

Fear can create strong signals, such as when you are caught in a fire or being attacked. It can also arise in non-dangerous situations such as exams, public speaking, being on a date, or trying to network with people you don't know at all. It is the feeling of being overwhelmed or feeling unable to cope with emotional and physical pressure.

So why do we cover suddenly the topic of fear? Because fear might get in your way to take action. So, to avoid that we need to know how to cope with it.

What is the impact of fear on our body?

Yes, we go into either fight or flight mode.

And what other physical effects does fear create?

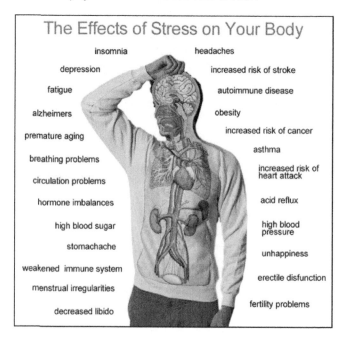

Fear or anxiety – what is the difference?

Anxiety is a type of fear. The things we described in the illustration opposite are also applicable to anxiety. The word anxiety describes worry or fear which is nagging and persists over time. It is used when the fear is about something in the future rather than what is happening now.

Fear and anxiety can last for a short time and then pass, but they can also last much longer, and you can get stuck with them. In some cases, these feelings can even take over your life. This can hold you back from doing things you want or need to do, which might impact more widely on your life as well.

What makes us afraid? Fearing failure can make you try to do well so that you won't fail, but it can also have the opposite effect. It can make you stop even trying something.

These feelings will vary from person to person. Just knowing what makes you afraid and why you need to continue to take the first steps is already a great start towards your goal.

Fear may be a one-off feeling when you are faced with something unfamiliar. It can, though, also be an everyday, long-lasting inhibitor as well.

Why am I talking about these strong feeling like stress, anxiety and fear?

Because these feelings are holding you back from moving ahead and might prevent you from taking action and taking charge of your professional life. I felt that it is important that we focus on this topic.

Coping with fear, anxiety and stress

Enough of the symptoms and insights, now, how can you cope with fear, anxiety or stress if they occur?

Here are some simple steps:

1. Know what triggers you
2. Face your fears
3. Plan ahead and get organized
4. Do one thing at a time
5. Manage expectations
6. Only set goals that are realistic and achievable
7. Change the way you view stress
8. Get enough good-quality downtime, rest and sleep
9. Let off steam

Treat yourself well.

And the most important element, never give up. You might not be able to take the first steps immediately. However, each step counts, each action counts.

And even if you fear something, do it nonetheless.

Let's deep dive a bit more into the points mentioned above.

1. Know what triggers you

Observe yourself – is it the thought of failing, not being successful, not being accepted, trying something you have never tried before? How should you cope with rejection?

Once you know what is triggering you, and it might not be easy to assess this immediately, so you might need assistance from a mentor or coach, you will be able to face your fears in a skilful way.

2. Face your fears

It can be difficult to get rid of fears. This is because they are rooted in our subconscious and appear instinctively and automatically.

Instead of focusing on how to get rid of them, a better approach is to focus on how you can work with them.

There are many methods to help with facing your fears. I would like to share one of them with you.

Slow Drip exposure
If you have a fear of public speaking, you might start building up your experience of public speaking over time. You might start off by presenting first to your family, then to your broader family, your friends, then go out and make a short presentation during a team meeting. The more you expose yourself to public speaking, the more you will notice and record the outcome. Notice the reception of your presentation to your audience. The more you do it the more you will be overcoming your fear.

The same for any situation in which you need to move forward.

3. Plan and get organised

I will be walking you through the planning phase in more detail in the next chapter.

Briefly, the more you write down when, which date or by when you would like to accomplish certain steps the more likely that it will get done. Stay tuned for the next chapter!

4. Do one thing at a time

Let's face it, you have only one brain and two hands. So, you can't do everything at the same time and if you try multi-tasking, the outcome may well not be to the high standard you would like it to be. You might need to revisit what you have done; this becomes double the time spent on the same task and therefore a waste of time. Better use of your valuable commodity, which is your time, is to focus on one task. Even if it is a telephone call, or just to write 5 sentences, whatever it is, if it is focused, it will be worth it. The magic wand here is again to do, to start, to just do something...

5. Manage expectations

We have high expectations of ourselves, of what we would like to do and accomplish. The human brain wants to have it all, which is great, and this is how it should be! "Shoot for the stars." However, the reality is that we can't do everything at once. Putting pressure on yourself will not help you at all. On the contrary, it will create stress, anxiety and in the end, you might not even be able to take a step forward as it has all become too much for you. You basically block. Lower your expectations. Not for the overall, ultimate goal, but for the steps would like to take for the day, week or month. That's why realistic planning and goal setting is so important. Split the big elephant in front of you into small pieces. Sometimes life gets in our way. It creates hurdles for us. You might need to support your family, or another unexpected urgent issue arises. You can't clone yourself, you can't do it all, and so setting priorities is key in those circumstances. At the end of the day, no one is going to die if you cannot complete the planned and desired action that week. Remember, it is your plan, and you can shift it around. What is crucial is that you don't lose sight of your steps and that you do complete the task, even if it is one week or month later, but you do it.

6. Only set goals which are realistic and achievable

Which brings us to the point of goal setting. We have already spoken about the importance of SMARTER goals:

S – Specific
M – Measurable
A – Achievable
R – Realistic
T – Time bound
E – Exciting
R – Results orientated

With that in mind, set your goals in such a manner that you CAN accomplish them on your own terms and circumstances. And that might be only making a phone call, writing an email, reading some research, or asking a friend. Each step counts. Always add a date – when do you want to have it done by, to hold yourself accountable.

It is your ballgame and no one else's. And ask for help if it seems too overwhelming, as someone from outside has a different perspective and can give you inspiration. That could be from your friends, peers, alumni, or a coach.

7. Change the way you view stress

There are two types of stress: good stress and bad stress.

Bad stress can impact negatively on your mind, body and soul.

The impact has been shown on the diagram on page 82.

However, there is good stress as well. Basically, this triggers the hormone adrenalin and that can cause excitement and joy.

Change your perspective and your perception of stress. See stress as your friend. As a great emotion to live with, something you can't wait to use to share with people your new message, your new service, ask questions, submit to an interview etc. For example, if you need to stand up and make a presentation about your services to your target audience, and you feel stress, see this as a great opportunity to raise your profile and to share something you feel passionate about.

8. Get enough good quality down-time, rest and sleep

Take good care of yourself. You are important, you are worth it. If you don't feel good, you can't be of use to anyone – not to yourself and neither to your job and what you would like to achieve and, more importantly, to the people surrounding you.

You are the priority – the rest will come.

9. Let off steam

If you feel the burden of frustration, failure or any other negative emotions that might and will come up, get them out. And you are the best person to know what is good for you. That might be taking a walk, talking to a friend, preparing a meal, reading, even going out into the forest and shouting. This is important, because if you leave it all inside you, it will pile up and create such a burning volcano that it will eventually just explode. And it will explode at a time and in a situation which has got nothing to do with that situation or the person you are with. Everyone, yourself included, will then be surprised why you have reacted in this way in a situation that is not worth It. In fact, all this is just the piling up of the negative emotions that need to get out, and if they are not articulated or dealt with at that time, they will create more outbursts at inappropriate times.

Imagine a glass of water, which is slowly filling up, and you feel it is going to overflow at some point. It just needs that one extra little drop of water that will trigger that to happen and then the water will start spilling over the glass. Feelings are like that. A better approach is to deal with them immediately, talk them over, and take a step back.

Summary

Everyone has fears, and the perspective and approach to deal with them is different from person to person. The main point is to face them. The more you face them, do something anyway, the more the fear will decrease and slowly turn into more positive emotions, because what you experience will be the opposite of your fears.

Be aware of your fears. Always have in mind though that when you do what you fear, what is the worst that can happen. The first attempt is always the hardest and at the same time the most courageous one.

I would like to share my personal story about my very first presentation in front of a crowd:

When I was working at the multinational company as a team manager, I had never made a town hall presentation in front of 600 people. One of my managers suggested me as a guest speaker to present the newly formed 'Diversity and Inclusion' stream, which I was leading. My first reaction was fear, but at the same time I was excited and proud that I had been given that opportunity. I created the presentation and did many rehearsals with my peers, how to stand in front of the audience, practised my voice, what to say or not, what to include, and the structure of the speech. After I don't how many training sessions, the D-Day was there and I had stomach ache, my heart was pounding, and I repeated what I was going to say over and over in my head.

Now it was my turn, and I took the microphone. I started to speak, and it felt like it was not me talking but someone else and that I was watching myself from outside. I did something that I had been given as a suggestion during my rehearsals from my peer. I started to talk and walk along the aisle and, guess what, every person started to follow me with their heads and eyes. I continued talking though. I can't tell you the sensation I had as I saw the interest, but I became so excited that I forgot half of what I wanted to say but the audience did not notice of course.

I finished my talk, and after the town hall, many people came up and congratulated me for an interesting and different style of talk and to find out more about the D&I stream I had created.

Take that leap of faith.

Don't forget, if you have something to share which is valuable and is something you believe in, then take the decision to step up in your professional life.

CHAPTER 9

THE IMPORTANCE OF PLANNING

We have prepared our mind, our soul, our body and made our decision. And we have all the tips and tricks in our toolbox – we know how to position, whom to reach out to. We have our own personal branding, our vision for ourselves, we know exactly who we are or almost. We know our strengths and values.

This is all great, but if we don't put that all into action, it will still not bring us anything.

And to be systematic is a good approach.

This does not mean that if you set out a plan and it does not go according to plan that you have failed.

What is the purpose of planning?

It helps keep you from spending time on tasks that won't bring you closer to your goal. **Planning your life gives you control.** If you create a plan then you get to make choices and decisions, rather than leaving things up to chance, or worse still, letting others make decisions for you.

Why is planning important in our daily lives?

- Planning is important to stay focused on the goals despite the constant change in situations around us.
- One small and crazy idea can become a big reality one day, just with proper planning. An example I like to give is the inspiring Shaukat Khanum Memorial Cancer Hospital & Research Centre in Pakistan. Here is a brief summary of that story:

Shaukat Khanum

Hailing from a family of proficient cricketers, and one Sufi Warrior Poet for an ancestor, Shaukat Khanum was a woman who was proud of her heritage. Hers was a pride she instilled in her five children, along with dignity and an iron resolve. In February 1985, Shaukat Khanum's family lost her to cancer. She was 63 years old. Imran Khan was her only son.

For Imran Khan, the devastation of his mother's death was secondary to watching her suffer through her struggle with cancer. The ordeal revealed a jarring reality: Pakistan had a dearth of medical resources when it came to treating cancer and this was costing lives. During the time spent with his mother in cancer wards, Imran Khan also witnessed the distress of other patients. He was especially troubled by those with limited means. How, he questioned, do the poor cope with a disease that is so debilitating to patients and their families? After his mother passed away, Imran Khan decided that irrespective of their background, everyone deserved an equal chance at life.

If you want to know more, you can google it. For reference here is the link: https://www.ikca.org.uk/about-ikca/background/

- An idea is nothing more than brain waves if there is no plan to execute it.
- Planning provides speed, competitive advantages, confidence, direction, and flexibility to fulfil your dream.

- Planning helps to direct and redirect the future for yourself and others, to help you to achieve the standard of living you are striving for. For example, if in future you need money immediately, what you will do? That's why most people save money, so that they can walk towards the future confidently. That's why planning is important to survive in life.

A good plan requires certain basic things and conditions, including duration, time management, daily, weekly and monthly actions and activities, what to do after achieving profit, what to do in the face of loss etc. It involves a great deal of brainstorming and think-tank work.

You need to remember that any plan can fail, and an expert can fail in planning. Planning is no guarantee of success, but it does help you to focus on your goal and create a structure that reduces the burden on your brain on a daily basis.

Planning your life is one of the most powerful and effective ways to attain what you want.

Think about this for a second, if:

- You travel, you plan your trip.
- You are getting married, you plan your wedding.
- You throw a party, you plan the event.
- You want to make more money, you plan for it.
- You want to be happy, you will do some planning.
- You want to be healthy, you surely make some plans for this.
- You want to lose weight, you set up some tasks for this.
- You want to travel and see the world, you will definitely plan for this.
- You want to have meaningful and happy relationships, then you must do some planning.

You would not dream of doing any of the above without some form of prior planning. Living a life of success filled with meaning, happiness and fulfilment is no different. Yet most people neglect to plan their lives and then get disappointed and discouraged when they do not attain what they want.

Your planning can be applied to both small and large aspects of your life. It could be that:

- You want to wake up earlier
- You're trying to stop bad habits
- You want to start your own business
- You want to lose weight
- You are aiming for a promotion or a better job

Planning steps

- The first step to planning is to clearly define your goals. Taking a few minutes to write down your goals will be highly beneficial.
- Once you have defined your goal, it is time to brainstorm the tasks required. Arrange all the necessary tasks into an order and assign an estimated time for the completion of each goal when you begin scheduling these activities.
- Next, it is useful to define the roles that you will take in fulfilling your goal as well as the roles of any others who will be assisting you. This is important, to avoid duplicating activity or causing confusion. Who will be assisting? Your Board of Directors, your network and your close family and friends.
- Once you have determined your goal, the tasks required, the key players and the tasks they will complete, it is finally time to start your scheduling. When scheduling, it is important to plan a weekly schedule as well as a daily one. The weekly schedule is important for the overall success of the project, but it is the daily planning that will help you to track your progress and determine whether you are on schedule.
- As the work starts, continually evaluate your performance to determine whether you are on track or need to adjust your schedule. This is where daily planning becomes so important.
- Finally, once you have successfully completed your task, review your planning process to determine how successful it was. This will help you by showing whether you have achieved an optimal planning process.

In my life, I can clearly see how planning is beneficial to me. When I have a plan to follow, I can check that I am on the path to success or not.

Advantages of planning

- Planning your life gives you control. If you create a plan then you get to make choices and decisions, rather than leaving things up to chance, or worse still, letting others make decisions for you.
- It becomes easier for you to identify and focus on your priorities when you create a plan because we all have multiple responsibilities and priorities in our lives.
- Planning helps to make your dreams more attainable. Once a realistic plan is in place, you will be amazed at how achievable your dreams really can be.
- Having a sense of purpose can go a long way to making you happier. A plan can help you establish your purpose. Once your plan is in place and you start putting it into action, you will no longer just "exist", you will instead "live purposefully."
- A plan will make it easier to say "No" to things that are not as important to you. In other words, if an opportunity is not aligned with your plan, then it's not worth your time right now and you can feel free to say "No" to it without any hesitation.
- A planned life will give you a sense of peace. You will no longer have to worry about whether you are making the correct decisions.
- Having a plan will make you feel more powerful. It not only gives you permission to live your life according to how you want, but it also gives you the tools to do it.
- Finally, having a plan ensures that you will have no regrets when you get to the end. Because you have made the effort to plan your life to achieve the goals that you want to achieve, so long as you stick to your plan you can be confident that you will not be looking backwards.

The question might come up, what to use as a planner? Well, there are so many digital resources out there. I use 'Trello', which allows you to create your own boxes of actions, and archive and categorize them.

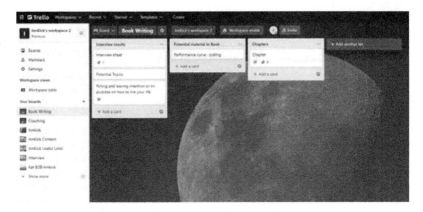

You can even store useful links, and ideas which come to your mind, and actions. However, explore for yourself what will work best for you.

You might choose to be more traditional and write things down in a specific book, or list everything on Excel.

All this requires hard work and focus. "From nothing comes nothing", so as you have made the decision to make a change (if you have), I am sure you will set aside the 10 minutes needed to take that first small step to get ahead.

And you might think, where shall I find the time? My schedule is overloaded already, and I can't even spend some personal time on myself. How am I supposed to do all this?

It's time to prioritise

Even though you can't do everything at once, prioritising helps you to figure out which tasks are the most important and which tasks can wait. If you know how to prioritise, you will be able to break up your work into smaller pieces. Then you can focus on each task, one at a time, starting with the most important.

Have you a million things to do? Create a list of everything you need to do. Then arrange the list in order, starting with the most important. Start tackling the things on your list in the order you have created.

Time management

There is no way to increase the time you have, but you can find ways to better use your time. Time management is making sure your actions help you finish the things you need to do. As you get better at managing your time, it will feel like you have more time.

A time management trick goes hand-in-hand with your list of priorities. With your list of priorities, add time estimates for each task on your list:

- Reply to emails – 20 minutes
- Meet with Sara – 60 minutes
- Pick up shopping – 20 minutes

Do your time estimates add up to far more time than you have? If so, re-prioritise. What can be moved or shrunk? Being as honest as possible will help you plan a more successful day.

I call this the 'Chuck It or Bucket List'.

Your Bucket List is what is important for you to do. On the Chuck It List should be things that you don't like or want to do. Are they necessary to do? Can you live without doing this? Then Chuck It... For example, watching some Netflix series you are just randomly following or skimming through Instagram or TikTok in the evening. That will require you to say NO as well... You don't know how to say NO?? I know, this is a difficult one. I still have issues with this as well. That is a subject for the next section.

Delegating and coordinating resources

Whether you recognise it or not, you have many resources around you. These start with your family, friends and also peers.

Assess whether the most unwanted task can be done by someone else. That could be cooking or shopping. Ask your partner if they can help to do the shopping once a week, as an example. Ask your kids if they can take care of their own room and clean it... Well, that may mean it does not get cleaned all the time as you would want it to be, and according to your standards, but who cares, if it is acceptable? Yes, go with it. It does not need to be perfect. And praise them as they take on tasks and complete them, to encourage them to continue. Cooking, which is essential for the whole family and yourself. How can you organize that very important task? Order a takeaway pizza once a week to save some time/pre-cook over the weekend and put it in the freezer. You don't need to cook healthily all the time, sometimes we just don't have time. Trust me, no one will complain.

At work or home, have your internal team with you on your journey and share with them what you would like to do. Make it clear that you might need more time and ask for their support. You will be amazed what the reaction will be. They will be wholeheartedly committed to helping you. Don't exclude them from your thought process either. Ask them for their feedback and comments. I can't emphasize enough how important this is.

As I started to write this book, I told my son about the project, and he encouraged me. He is sometimes reading chapters and giving me feedback or feedforward. He is always asking how it is going, so he keeps me accountable. We chose my book cover design together. It made him happy to be involved and help mummy out. And it helped me to have an extra pairs of eyes.

So, I changed the name of feedback to feedforward, why? Because any comment, criticism and suggestions are a way forward for you.

Practise feeding forward too with your peers and your managers, depending on where you are in your journey and who you have assessed to help you.

Plan as much as you can. There will be always something that comes up to get in your way. Parents visiting, being sick, having a new assignment. This is life but that should not let you deviate from your overall goal and the steps you have put in place. You might take a break, but then come back on track.

Visit your plan again, adjust the timings and start working on it.

Motto: **Never Give Up**

- What small thing are you going to do?
- When and how are you going to do it?
- Who and what can help you to achieve it?
- What could get in your way?
- How are you going to overcome that obstacle?
- What is the level of your commitment?
- How much do you believe that you are going to do what you say?

Start your brainstorm and enjoy it, have fun. You can be creative. Draw, or video, whatever is good for you.

CHAPTER 10

HOW TO SAY NO

This is about not only saying no, but also being equipped to decline meetings, and avoid unnecessary actions and tasks. It is about being selective in what you would like to do and what you need to do.

This is particularly important if you are working full-time, have family commitments and yet would still like to implement some changes in your professional life.

After the planning stage, to be able to take action, you need to carve out time. Each day, we have only 24 hours available. You need to take care of yourself, your family and friends, not to mention your current workload.

How can you carve out time?

You need to set boundaries. Where and with whom and what?

With your friends, family and peers.

Observe where you spend time during the day. Which activities can you do without? Identify meetings, gatherings or unofficial chats that you can decline to spend time on. Try to limit spending time on too many chit-chats during the day so that you can still perform all your tasks, while still taking your steps towards your goals. Specifically, if you want to make a move within your company, you need to spend time networking, in lunch meetings or having Zoom meetings with the people who can help you advance. The key here is: with intention.

If you want to move to a different industry or company, you need to get involved in some outside networking, attend webinars and start to connect with people – reach out, write, connect over LinkedIn. That means finding time for these outside your working hours or after or before work or during lunch.

Make a realistic plan. Certain actions can be taken once a week, bi-weekly or monthly. Or some of them can be taken over the weekend.

Ask for help from your family.

Include your partner in your plan and what you would like to achieve. Ask your partner for assistance to take on some household duties. Even just a small task taken from you will be beneficial. Your kids can help you as well.

If you have set time aside in the evening once a week for your actions, tell everyone that you are not to be disturbed. Make sure you have quality and focused time. If you can focus even for just 30 minutes, you will get so much done that you can't believe it.

Be firm but polite. Be clear and direct. That might sound a bit selfish, which it is, but you need to have this selfish time to be able to reach your goal.

Otherwise, the plan you have made will be only a wish list. We need to aim to take concrete action.

Remember, there will never be a good moment, a perfect time to start. Life will throw up barriers and this is normal. You need to have your goals in front of you every day, a vision board like we explained in previous chapters. Or get into the habit of checking your action plan.

But don't get paranoid about it either. I would like you to have fun and enjoy the process. It should not feel like torture.

It's time to delegate

- Think about who else can help you in achieving certain tasks.
- Friends and peers are good to start with.
- Always be clear and honest on what you expect from them. Don't let them guess.
- What can you delegate to them? There is always something that can be handed over.

To give you some ideas:

- Proofreading your email or a letter of proposal
- Introducing you to someone
- Writing an email
- Analysing reports, compiling lists
- Helping out with website updates and social media posts

These are just a few examples of where you can ask for help.

By setting boundaries, being clear and direct, you will set things up well for yourself. You will be more productive and have peace of mind.

To start with, you might feel guilty but try to push that thought away. Your subconscious will be overruling your conscious mind as it is used to going down the same path.

But you have the willpower of your brain, and you can choose which path to take. Take it wisely. You are smarter and you know how your brain wants to trick you. You need to plan and eliminate actions depending on whether they will be useful for you to spend time on. It is now all about intentions, with purpose, with a goal in mind.

Every new experience is valuable

Sometimes, events or chats you spend with someone whom you think is just a waste of time, can turn out to be extremely valuable. The people you meet might have connections, the required network or information you are looking for. If you don't invest the time, you will never know.

I try each path. I have at least one meeting, one lunch or attend a webinar which I am not even sure will give me the desired results. At first glance you might say that I am contradicting myself about using time wisely, and yes, to some extent, I am. Time is precious – it is our most precious commodity and once it is used it cannot be retrieved. But you need to try things out in order to succeed.

Each individual is different and unique. I am a curious person, hence I am always trying to get to know different people, attend webinars, go to networking events, sometimes with a vague idea that I might get to know some interesting people. And sometimes I do and sometimes I don't.

For me this is never a waste of time. It is more a new experience, a new try which did not turn out as I envisaged. However, I am not harsh on myself and don't judge at all.

You need to adopt the same outlook. Whether you want to create a more rigid and focused plan or like me be a bit more flexible is up to you.

Ultimately, you need to manage your time wisely, if you want to fit in your daily job, family, personal leisure and also prompt a change in your career.

Changing career, moving up, or changing industry is a real job. It is a job on top of your day-to-day one, thus it requires time, planning, and determination.

Determination is key to success

What else can you do to say NO?

Think about whether you would rather like to spend time working on your professional journey or spend time otherwise.

If you do so, be aware that some tasks will be delayed or you need to spend time during the night, over the weekend or early in the morning.

It is really about how much you are willing to sacrifice. Sacrifice is a heavy word, and you are supposed to have fun, but there is always a price to be paid.

During my professional life, we had many parties, dinners and then went out clubbing or to a bar. That meant that we were really late going to bed, even when the next day we had to work. Some peers decided to leave the party early, while some, like me, stayed until the end, yet still I was at work in the morning, right on time at 07.30am, opening up the office. I am an early bird. Did I get enough sleep? No, of course not. This was the price I paid for that day. But I chose and I knew that it would be like that. I have always survived, with plenty of coffees and early sleep the next evening. I am aware that this is not suitable for everyone. You have the choice – you are in the driver's seat and you decide for yourself. That might be choosing to go to the party, or not. Make sure that you have a balance that fits your own circumstances.

In the same way, you can filter what to say NO to and what to say YES to.

What I am sharing is how to assist you to make the decisions which are appropriate for you as a person.

You have the full potential to do everything you plan for.

To recap

- Assess what you can live without doing
- Ask for help from your family, friends and peers
- Choose wisely and with purpose, with a goal in mind. It's your choice
- Your time is precious
- You can be selfish, don't feel guilty

Have your goal in mind. It is overwhelming when thinking about all that you need to do. But your step-by-step guide and plan will help you to see and measure how much you have done. Always congratulate yourself for each step you take even if that may only be one step each week. It does not matter.

Sometimes you need to say NO to a cinema outing or you need to work over the weekend, on Sunday morning a bit to catch up with your tasks.

Without investment of time, there will be no reward.

The results will not come immediately. Be prepared to wait and be patient.

Plant the seeds wherever you can. Which one of them will bear fruit, you will never know. My famous quote.

Don't get annoyed at yourself if any effort seems to feel useless, or some recurring catch-up meetings do not serve your purpose.

Create space for some reflection time. Reflection helps you to internalise your learnings, to absorb what you have just read or watched or heard. Great leaders are great readers and writers.

Here are your reflection questions:

- What small thing you are going to do?
- When and how are you going to do it?
- Who and what can help you to achieve it?

- What could get in your way?
- How are you going to overcome that obstacle?
- What is the level of your commitment?
- How much do you believe that you are going to do what you say?

The Disney recipe for clear thinking

Let's try out a very famous coaching model.

Yes, we are talking about Walt Disney, the filmmaker, Mickey Mouse, Dumbo, all those animated films. He is quoted as saying:

"If you dream it, you can do it."

Here I would like to introduce you to a different way of validating your plan. It is widely used in coaching.

In the Disney recipe there are 3 roles/positions/mindsets:

- Dreamer – dreams up ideas
- Realist – makes things happen
- Critic – evaluates and refines

This strategy is used in coaching as well as in corporates to inspire employees and leaders.

Walt Disney was not an easy manager/leader. However, he motivated his team and the results of this can be seen in all his films.

When he decided to make a new film, he visited first the 'Dreamer' team, to tell them his draft idea and let the team build on it with some crazy brainstorming. At this stage, everything is possible, with no constraints. Like Dumbo the flying elephant.

Once the 'Dreamer' team had finished their mind-blowing brainstorm, Walt Disney went to see his second team, the 'Realistic' and asked them: this is the idea for the film, what do you think? How can we get this done? The Realistic team started to think about the practicalities, budget, resources, audience and how to put that into action. Basically, they created the boring (but necessary!) stuff, the project plan.

Once that was done, Walt went to see his third team, 'Critical'. They had the responsibility to think about what the obstacles could be, what was needed to be considered, and any other constraints that needed to be thought about.

Once that was done, he went again to see the Dreamers to ask, OK, here we have both sides of the coin, how crazy can we be? And voila, the new film had been created. Of course, this is easier said than done. However, this coaching or thinking model is used to great effect, along with some caveats to accommodate the reality of each specific project.

Robert Dilts has studied Disney and especially his methods for guaranteeing maximum creativity. These methods have been transformed into a life and business coaching method, which is commonly called the 'Disney Strategy' or 'Disney Coaching'.

How can we put this into practice and how can you use it for your decision-making process?

Assign 3 different locations in the same room or even in different rooms:

1. Dreamer
2. Realistic
3. Critical

Write these titles down on paper or use different objects to create these spaces for you.

Start with spot 1, the Dreamer. Here you can go wild with your dreams.

- Become the "what if..." possibility thinker.
- What do I want?
- What will I be doing – and where will I be doing it?
- What are the benefits of achieving this?
- What will this mean for me as a person?
- How will it benefit those who are close to me?

Once you have finished visualising your Dreamer position, move to your second spot, Realistic. This is your planning stage and so ask yourself these questions:

- How can I make this dream happen?
- What are the main chunks or sections of this dream? How do they follow one another?
- What steps must I take to make each chunk happen?
- Why is this step necessary? And this one? And this one?
- What resources (time, people, money etc) do I need to make it happen?
- What will I see and hear that will be evidence that each chunk has been achieved?
- What will I see and hear that will be evidence that the dream has been achieved?

Last but not least, you arrive on spot 3, Critical or the 'Constructive Critic'. Here, we don't want to delete the whole plan but it is the place to scrutinise it and ask some tough questions:

- What are the weaknesses in this plan?
- What is missing?
- What is inappropriate?
- What problems could occur?
- Who might object? Who will be unfavourably affected by this?
- When and where might this not work? Or not be desirable?
- Any other weaknesses in this plan?

Circle back around through 1, 2 and 3 again, if necessary, to go back over your plan for your future. These techniques might help you in making the right decision and in putting it into action. You can ask for help from someone to ask you the questions listed above, allowing you to just think about the answers, which may make the process a bit easier. Rinse and repeat as much as you need.

Get your friends, peers helping you with posing the questions. At first this model seems to be awkward but once you did several times, you will see how your mind is opening up and how you can validate and put into action your goal.

CHAPTER 11

RECAP

What have you learned?

We went through your possible career journey. Yours might not be the same but it is likely to resemble what we have described in some way.

We started with the excitement of starting your professional life, progressing, and coming to the point of stagnation.

Even you may not have noticed that you are stuck, as life is continuous in its fast pace, particularly when you have taken on additional responsibilities.

In the meantime, the company might have changed, merged with another enterprise, meaning that the culture is not the same anymore. Management likewise. It starts to become a toxic environment.

Or it could be that everything is the same, also with your position, and there is no moving ahead in prospect – it is getting boring. You don't feel fulfilled anymore.

This is your hamster wheel. This is the point where we start to analyse your values. I explained how you can put that value elicitation in place using the interactive exercises in the book appendices.

Then we moved to the decision tree. With the challenging questions, you will determine what is right for you. Have you done that already? Do you know where you are with your decision? That will have formed the foundation for taking the next steps.

I introduced the STAR model. This model is a framework to list your accomplishments, talk about your success in an objective and non-bragging way. Short and sweet.

Then I talked about support. The importance of identifying your support circle. With intention and meaning. Thus the significance of creating your board of directors according to your needs, who can vouch for you and sponsor you. And you need sponsors, as nobody can succeed alone.

And networking. As it states, it is work. In our day-to-day work we don't do enough networking, as we think it is not necessary. However, it is so vital that we spend time doing this, even if we are satisfied with our current job. Get out of your bubble with the same people, same peers, same company. Starting by mixing and mingling with different departments in the same company might feel a comfortable way to start. Have coffees or lunches with people outside your team. It is a great experience to get to know other peers and managers, listen to their life stories, tips and tricks on how to move on, or to get information about new connections. Either way, even if there is no real learning, these can be enriching encounters.

Within the company might feel easier, but you need to network outside as well. Thus, I introduced the Networking Wheel. Scan through your networking circle. Check to see how diverse it is and see who is missing. This will become the basis for your targeted networking. And you need to be consistent on increasing, maintaining and nurturing your expanding spiderweb. Sometimes, and particularly with the disruption from the pandemic, face-to-face networking is sometimes not possible, so how can we move this to a virtual platform? For professionals we have LinkedIn, the perfect virtual networking tool.

Did you invest in your LinkedIn profile? Invest in time and thought and creativity? Do you know all the ins and outs of LinkedIn?

I explained the basic and simple features but there is so much more to it than that. LinkedIn is highly sophisticated and powerful but at same time very user-friendly. And its power lies in that it is truly global, so you can connect with anyone in the world.

But before you do that, make sure you take action to improve your profile, to gain the maximum value from when people check you out. Even Human Resources will be checking you out.

If you want more detail information on using LinkedIn, you can always reach out to me.

Continuing with communication, assertive communication. This is not so much about what you say, it is about how you say it. So true. When connecting, your language and communication style is crucial.

I have provided some examples of how to use assertive communication. With this audience-appropriate communication style, you can convey bad, challenging and good news smoothly.

Can you describe the difference between a coach and a mentor? Their roles converge and yet at the same time are so different. Remind yourself of the different methodologies available to assist and support people.

Then there is one of the most important ingredients: Grit

This requires constant practising, constant learning, and exercise. Even though life will throw at you some challenges, still you should not lose your focus and you must carry on. Just like top athletes do, and in my chapter, I gave an impactful technique as well of breathing that you can apply to practise Grit.

Grit is required for a winning attitude, whatever you would like to win.

So far, what are your key takeaways that you can start to work on?

Have you planned already? Take this moment to reflect. Take a notebook, paper, or write on your PC.

Growth mindset: that is a powerful phrase but at same time so intimidating. Overwhelming.

In Chapter 7 I have outlined for you the 10 key characteristics of a growth mindset. In essence, it is about being flexible, open-minded and curious. To have the courage to try new things. Trying is learning, trying is moving a step ahead, knowing more than before.

I gave you as well one NLP technique that you can use anywhere: anchoring. Very powerful for rewiring your brain.

All of the above is great but you need to have the basic skills to change to either a new profession, new department or to start your own business. How will you know what are missing as skills?

Very simply, get in touch with people who are either doing it, are in that industry or are entrepreneurs. Learn from them what is essential. The best way is to spend some time, and that could be one hour or more if you have that time, shadowing the person doing it.

In the appendices you will find a list of aptitudes and skills, where you can evaluate yourself about what is needed for the mastery of the certain skills. You don't need to evaluate all of them, only the ones which are applicable. By doing so, you can see what is needed.

I added one more NLP technique – that of how to learn from the experts. Can you learn all the tips and tricks? No, of course not. However, it will give you an indication about which route to take or proceed on. Can you learn on the job, yes, for sure. But you need to have the basics to be eligible to apply for the job. You don't need to be 100% so don't play the safe card and not apply if you don't tick every box, but you need to be able to show some sort of certification or level of attainment and demonstrate your soft skills and experience. Ultimately you can speak to your Human Resources department as well to know more.

It's time to talk about what is holding you back. One of the factors is FEAR, fear of failing, fear of making a fool of yourself.

Fear is a powerful feeling and overtakes your common sense. It is buried in the unconscious mind, the influence of which is so strong. And the influence of others on you. If you share your thoughts with your family, friends and peers, they might want to convince you that everything is OK as it is. Why would you change and paint a picture which is negative? What will happen if you don't succeed? You will lose money, reputation, your job. You have responsibilities. All these thoughts will play on your brain. How to cope with fear is explained in Chapter 8.

Coming back to the comments of others. If you have made up your mind and you have that burning passion inside you, no one can influence you unless you allow them to. This is where we have Chapter 10 to showcase how to say NO. Not only to tasks, jobs, and setting new priorities but also to people who don't listen to you or people who don't want to understand you. Being critical and asking difficult questions stimulates your mind. Be selective with whom you are going to share your thoughts. Seek out people who can be objective but at same time supportive.

All the above is nothing without a plan and this is explained in Chapter 9. Time management is key as well as prioritisation and which tasks you can afford to leave undone and which ones are essential.

You can make use of different software applications which have free plans. I use Trello for my project planning and listing down my thoughts and useful links. I presented a screenshot of that. There are many planning tools to choose from, or you might be traditional and simply use Excel or Word. It is important that you make a list, a step-by-step guide for the week. Don't be too harsh on yourself and be kind. Be realistic. Rome was not built in one day either. Each step counts. Make the utmost effort to complete each step. We know life is unpredictable, anything can happen, and we might not be able to act. Under normal circumstances though, make sure you do it. Which brings us to procrastination, as this is all-too easy to do. Delaying and postponing activities we don't want to do, or we deem too difficult or new or unknown territory. Like hiding from the bad news or being like an ostrich which puts its head in the sand, this just leaves the rest of the body open to getting hurt.

Mindset shift plays a huge role here. How can you be motivated to take that action? You need to visualise the results in front of you if you are planning to take a certain action. What feeling you will have, as being aware of what we will feel is so important. Imagine how it will feel once you have reached out to that person and have an appointment for lunch. Is that not great to see, feel and hear?

Here we have the vision board which might help you.

What type are you?

- Visionary
- Feeling
- Hearing
- Kinaesthetic

Have you ever thought about this? Are you using in your language more words such as seeing? Or are you more sensitive to feelings? What is your learning style? Some people need to read, some need to do, some need to see.

Why is that important?

This is one of your motivators.

Once you have identified this and you can get help from your friends, peers, family, or a professional coach, you can build a motivation plan for yourself.

If you are more visionary, a vision board is spot on, or pictures of what success will look like. Or where you see yourself in five years for example.

If you are more of a feeling person, you might want to imagine the feelings at the end, the sensation of the feeling that you acted.

If you are more the kinaesthetic type, you need to touch stuff, you need to do stuff. Real action is your thing. Just reading does not do it for you.

And how can you beat procrastination?

Think ahead about what could be coming in your way: kids, unplanned tasks, lack of sleep, day-to-day job pressures, even overwhelm.

Make a list of these and anticipate how often this could happen and how you could overcome this.

Each time you are tempted to postpone a task, check out your list and remind yourself what to do.

And don't forget the importance of feedback. On how you did in the interview, with the presentation or speech. Or facilitating the meeting. I changed the name of feedback to feedforward, as any comments will bring you one step forward.

We all need to work, and we spend more time at work than with our families sometimes. Why not have a job which is fun, fulfilling, and enjoyable? Where you feel valued, where you can speak up and share your thoughts, where you are promoted and noticed, and where you have an impact.

As I mentioned at the beginning, you need to decide first what exactly you expect from your professional life. To stay or go? To stay and move up or to a different department? Or change completely the industry you are in or make a bold change by becoming an entrepreneur.

It is your life, and we live once. Live the fullest life, you deserve it, you are worth it, and you are doing well enough.

Here I would like to allude to positive affirmations and how they can support you in the morning to start your day with a strong intention. An intention to be happy, to have fun and seek joy, to be successful, it could be anything, any small thing is fine.

Affirmation is your own promise to yourself. Put it in your heart.

What is your affirmation, your personal pledge for today, tomorrow and for your future?

APPENDIX

Activity 1: Be clear on your values

Exercise 1: Determine your top 10 values

Based on your experiences of happiness, pride and fulfilment, using the following list of common personal values. (Tick 10)

Note: As you work through, you may find that some of these naturally combine. For instance, if you value philanthropy, community, and generosity, you might say that service to others is one of your top values.

☐ Accountability	☐ Excellence	☐ Perfection
☐ Accuracy	☐ Excitement	☐ Piety
☐ Achievement	☐ Expertise	☐ Positivity
☐ Adventurousness	☐ Exploration	☐ Practicality
☐ Altruism	☐ Expressiveness	☐ Preparedness
☐ Ambition	☐ Fairness	☐ Professionalism
☐ Assertiveness	☐ Faith	☐ Prudence
☐ Balance	☐ Family-orientatedness	☐ Quality-orientation
☐ Being the best	☐ Fidelity	☐ Reliability

☐ Belonging	☐ Fitness	☐ Resourcefulness
☐ Boldness	☐ Fluency	☐ Restraint
☐ Calmness	☐ Focus	☐ Results-oriented
☐ Carefulness	☐ Freedom	☐ Rigour
☐ Challenge	☐ Fun	☐ Security
☐ Cheerfulness	☐ Generosity	☐ Self-actualization
☐ Clear-mindedness	☐ Goodness	☐ Self-control
☐ Commitment	☐ Grace	☐ Selflessness
☐ Community	☐ Growth	☐ Self-reliance
☐ Compassion	☐ Happiness	☐ Sensitivity
☐ Competitiveness	☐ Hard work	☐ Serenity
☐ Consistency	☐ Health	☐ Service
☐ Contentment	☐ Helping Society	☐ Shrewdness
☐ Continuous improvement	☐ Holiness	☐ Simplicity
☐ Contribution	☐ Honesty	☐ Soundness
☐ Control	☐ Honour	☐ Speed
☐ Cooperation	☐ Humility	☐ Spontaneity
☐ Correctness	☐ Independence	☐ Stability
☐ Courtesy	☐ Ingenuity	☐ Strategic
☐ Creativity	☐ Inner harmony	☐ Strength
☐ Curiosity	☐ Inquisitiveness	☐ Structure
☐ Decisiveness	☐ Insightfulness	☐ Success
☐ Democratic	☐ Intelligence	☐ Support
☐ Dependability	☐ Intellectual status	☐ Teamwork
☐ Determination	☐ Intuition	☐ Temperance
☐ Devoutness	☐ Joy	☐ Thankfulness
☐ Diligence	☐ Justice	☐ Thoroughness
☐ Discipline	☐ Leadership	☐ Thoughtfulness
☐ Discretion	☐ Legacy	☐ Timeliness
☐ Diversity	☐ Love	☐ Tolerance
☐ Dynamism	☐ Loyalty	☐ Traditionalism
☐ Economy	☐ Making a difference	☐ Trustworthiness
☐ Effectiveness	☐ Mastery	☐ Truth-seeking
☐ Efficiency	☐ Merit	☐ Understanding
☐ Elegance	☐ Obedience	☐ Uniqueness
☐ Empathy	☐ Openness	☐ Unity
☐ Enjoyment	☐ Order	☐ Usefulness
☐ Enthusiasm	☐ Originality	☐ Vision
☐ Equality	☐ Patriotism	☐ Vitality

Exercise 2: Prioritise your top five values

Jot down your list of 10 values here:

1. _____

2. _____

3. _____

4. _____

5. _____

6. _____

7. _____

8. _____

9. _____

10. _____

Reduce your list of 10 values to the top five that are most important to you. Write down your top values, in order of importance with #1 meaning the highest priority value.

This step is probably the most difficult, because you'll have to look deep inside yourself. It's also the most important step, because, when deciding, you'll have to choose between solutions that may satisfy different values. This is when you must know which value is more important to you.

Helpful tip: If you struggle to determine which are your top five, do a comparison of each value (from above) until you have reached five. Ask yourself, "If I could satisfy only one of these, which would I choose?" If you can navigate through work and life without them, they are not your top five values.

1. _____

2. _____

3. _____

4. _____

5. _____

Exercise 3: Narrow down to your top three values

Reduce your list of five values to the top three that are most important to you to have and that you could not live without.

1. _____

2. _____

3. _____

Activity 2: Evaluate your skills

What are the talents and skills you possess that are most important to you and that you enjoy? Part of your mission statement should reflect your best aptitudes and strengths (what you list here in combination with the results of Activity 1). Remember, these aptitudes are what create joy and energy in your life. Use this assessment to rate your skills and to identify those that you want to develop. Rate your current level of proficiency from "1" (beginner level) to "5" (expert level). Some of the skills listed below may not apply to your career direction presently or in future, so simply skip those items. Fill in open fields with your skills that are not provided in the list.

DATE OF ASSESSMENT:

Skill	Level of Proficiency (1-5)	Capture personal reminders and notes. Key skills you want to develop, possible examples and/or when you will focus on them.
COMMUNICATION SKILLS		
Business writing		
Proposal writing		
Presentation		
Facilitation		
Running a meeting		
Listening		
Interviewing		
Influencing		

Skill	Level of Proficiency (1-5)	Capture personal reminders and notes. Key skills you want to develop, possible examples and/or when you will focus on them.
Giving and receiving feedback		
Conflict resolution		
Negotiating		
Creative or promotional writing		
Editing or copyediting		
Proofreading		
Writing job descriptions		
Other:		
TECHNOLOGY AND COMPUTER SKILLS		
Word processing		
Spreadsheets		
HTML, XML, and other programming skills		
Project management		
Presentation software		
Graphics software		
Other:		
FINANCIAL SKILLS		
Budgeting		

Skill	Level of Proficiency (1-5)	Capture personal reminders and notes. Key skills you want to develop, possible examples and/or when you will focus on them.
Financial analysis		
Cost accounting		
Forecasting		
Tracking and management		
Preparing a business plan		
Other:		
SUPERVISORY SKILLS		
Hiring		
Coaching		
Delegating		
Setting goals and objectives		
Assessing performance		
Leading		
Training and support development		
Analysing workflow and processes		
Recruiting and retention		
Administrative management		
Other:		

Skill	Level of Proficiency (1–5)	Capture personal reminders and notes. Key skills you want to develop, possible examples and/or when you will focus on them.
MANAGEMENT SKILLS		
Managing change		
Customers, internal and/or external		
Project management		
Production or implementation management		
Managing upward		
Solving business problems		
Business analysis, critical thinking		
Internal consulting and networking		
Vendor management		
Tactical planning		
Creative thinking, brainstorming		
Managing for innovation		
Other:		
TEAMWORK SKILLS		
Leading a team		
Group problem solving		
Keeping teams on target		

Skill	Level of Proficiency (1-5)	Capture personal reminders and notes. Key skills you want to develop, possible examples and/or when you will focus on them.
Working with a virtual team		
Assuming team membership roles		
Collaborating		
Other:		
SELF-MANAGEMENT SKILLS		
Self-awareness		
Emotional intelligence		
Time management		
Balancing work and life		
Career development		
Stress management		
Limit setting and goal setting		
Using power and authority positively		
Seeing multiple perspectives		
Other:		
SALES AND MARKETING SKILLS		
Product marketing		
Direct marketing		

Skill	Level of Proficiency (1-5)	Capture personal reminders and notes. Key skills you want to develop, possible examples and/or when you will focus on them.
Market research		
Telemarketing		
Promotions		
Publicity		
Electronic marketing		
Consumer marketing		
Business-to-business marketing		
Competitive analysis and planning		
Direct sales		
Sales forecasting		
Consultative selling		
Other:		
PHYSICAL AND MANUAL DEXTERITY SKILLS		
Assembling, constructing, or building		
Operating tools or machinery		
Fixing or repairing		
Ability to train others on tasks		
Assembling, constructing, or building		

Skill	Level of Proficiency (1-5)	Capture personal reminders and notes. Key skills you want to develop, possible examples and/or when you will focus on them.
Other:		
OTHER INDUSTRY AND/OR JOB-SPECIFIC SKILLS (LIST)		
1.		
2.		
3.		
4.		
5.		

Activity 3: Create your personal Board of Directors

Board of Directors list

Name of Prospective Member of Board of Directors	Area of Expertise	Type (Strategic, Operational, Developmental)	Role (Influencer, Connector)	What are his/her interests?	What do I have to offer?

Activity 4: Fill in your Wheel of Life

Fill in your own version of the Wheel of Life, scoring out of ten where you believe you are right now in each of the eight categories, as per the first version shown.

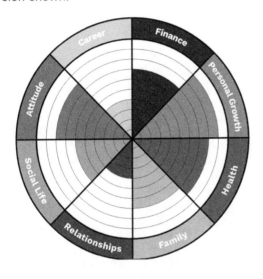

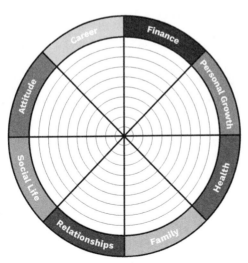

Activity 5: Complete your vision board

Here is a vision board I completed for my own use, which may inspire you when putting together your own one:

Activity 6: Complete your Personal Business Model Canvas

Answer the questions on this form to help you to develop your personal canvas:

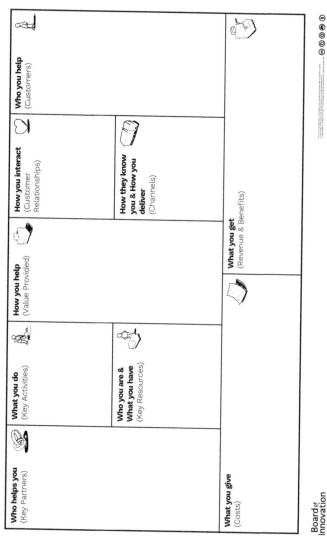

The Personal Business Model Canvas

Who helps you
(Key Partners)

What you do
(Key Activities)

Who you are &
What you have
(Key Resources)

How you help
(Value Provided)

How you interact
(Customer Relationships)

How they know
you & How you
deliver
(Channels)

Who you help
(Customers)

What you give
(Costs)

What you get
(Revenue & Benefits)

Board of Innovation

www.businessmodelgeneration.com

Activity 7: Entrepreneurs, complete your Business Model Canvas

Answer the questions on this form to help you to develop your business canvas:

PERSONAL BUSINESS MODEL

NAME: _____ DATE: _____

KEY PARTNERS:
WHO IS HELPING YOU?

KEY ACTIVITIES:
WHAT ARE YOU DOING?

KEY RESSOURCES:
WHAT DO YOU HAVE?
WHAT DO YOU NEED?

VALUE PROPOSITION:
HOW CAN YOU HELP?

CUSTOMER RELATIONSHIP:
HOW DO YOU INTERACT?

CHANNELS:
HOW DO PEOPLE KNOW YOU?

CUSTOMER SEGMENTS:
WHO ARE YOU HELPING?

COST STRUCTURE:
WHAT ARE YOU INVESTING?

REVENUE STREAMS:
WHAT DO YOU GET?

Activity 8: Map out your Networking Wheel

Map out your own version of the Networking Wheel of the individuals who are currently members of your network, as per the first version shown.

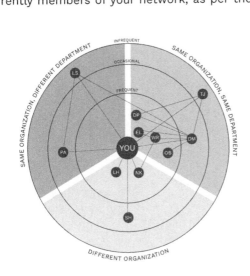

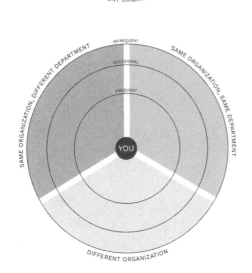

GET IN TOUCH

Want to learn more, or work with Hulya one-to-one to break free from *YOUR* hamster wheel? Here is how you can get in touch with her:

Web site: https://innkick.com

Email: hulya@innkick.com

Linkedin: https://www.linkedin.com/in/hulyakurt-innkick/

Facebook: https://www.facebook.com/hulya.kurt.3762/

Instagram: https://www.instagram.com/hulyakurt_coach/

Printed in Great Britain
by Amazon